Mastering

Microsoft Intune

Harness the Full Potential of Microsoft Intune for Seamless Device
Control & Unlock the Power of Cloud-Based Management for
Enhanced Security and Productivity

Aurora Cameron

TABLE OF CONTENTS

CHAPTER 1
ALL ABOUT MICROSOFT INTUNE

Introduction to Microsoft Intune

Microsoft Intune is a cloud-based service that lets you control mobile devices, mobile apps, and PCs. Without having to set up hardware on-site, it lets businesses control their devices and keep their data safe. Businesses can control devices like computers, smartphones, and tablets with Microsoft Intune, no matter what operating system they are using. One of the best things about Microsoft Intune is that it can make the user experience smooth and uniform across all devices. It's easy for users to get to business tools and apps, and companies can protect private data and apply security policies. Administrators can specify who can access which apps and files, ensuring that only people who are allowed to can see or change private data. Microsoft Intune also has a lot of security features to keep devices and data safe from possible risks. This lets companies make sure that even if a device is lost or stolen, the data is still safe by requiring encryption, passcodes, and remote wiping.

Intune also offers tracking and reporting in real-time, so managers can see any strange activity right away and take steps to reduce risks. Microsoft Intune not only has strong security features, but it also makes managing apps easier. Organizations can use it to share and update apps across multiple devices, ensuring that users have access to the most recent versions. Intune also works with both public and private app stores, so businesses can pick the one that works best for them when it comes to distributing apps. One cool thing about Microsoft Intune is that it works with other Microsoft services, like Azure Active Directory and Office 365. With this connection, businesses can easily control user IDs and resource access while ensuring that users have the same experience on all Microsoft platforms.

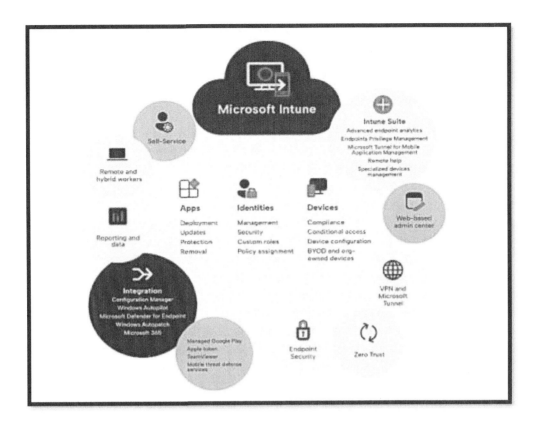

Understanding the Benefits of Microsoft Intune

Companies that want to control and protect their devices and data can get a lot out of Microsoft Intune:

- **Centralized Management:** You can easily set up and control policies, devices, and apps from a single console. This makes management easier and more effective.
- **Security Policy Enforcement:** Make sure security policies are followed and data is kept safe, even on devices that aren't owned by the company. To ensure data security, establish and implement policies like requiring a password, encrypting data, and limiting apps.
- **Device Management Flexibility:** Handle both company-owned and "bring your device" (BYOD) situations. Support a lot of different ways of owning devices while keeping control of company info and apps.
- **Advanced Threat Protection:** Features like restricted access and mobile threat defense can help protect you from new online risks. Real-time monitoring and action of possible security threats are needed to keep private data safe.
- **Comprehensive App Management:** With comprehensive app management, you can make it easier to install and handle apps. It is easy to share and update apps across devices

so that all employees can use the most up-to-date versions and features. This makes employees more productive and makes it easier for IT teams to handle apps.

- **Flexible Licensing Options:** You can pick the plan that best fits your needs from some flexible licensing options. Intune offers options that can grow with the needs of the organization, whether it's a small business or a large-scale corporation.

Features of Microsoft Intune

Enhanced Advanced Analytics Features

This tool lets you use the standard Kusto Query Language (KQL) syntax to ask about device data in real-time from individual Windows devices that are controlled in the cloud. It adds to the ability to see inventory data that has already been collected in Intune. By making a live link to the device and running questions in real-time, it improves usefulness by giving managers access to more information about the state and setup of the device. **Note:** You can get Microsoft Intune Advanced Analytics as a separate add-on or as part of the Intune Suite. The new features, like Device query and battery health reports will be added to the Intune Suite and the new Advanced Analytics add-on. These features will include the ability to find anomalies, see the history of devices, and see the whole scope of devices. Support staff, security experts, and IT managers can use real-time, detailed data from device questions to learn more about the hardware features and settings of devices. This lets them respond quickly to threats and other problems.

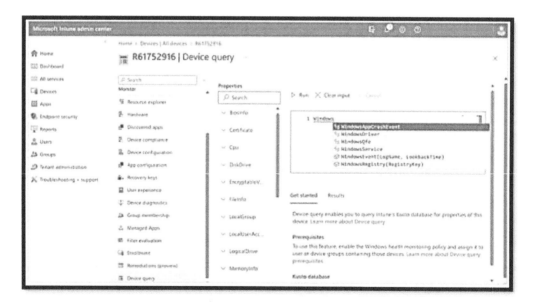

The Advanced Analytics Battery Health Report is now generally available (GA). This new report improves the asset management experience for IT workers by giving them more information, helping to avoid costly downtime, and giving them advice on what to buy. This report also works with license device scores, which helps IT managers quickly, find hardware problems like a dead battery that needs to be replaced before the guarantee runs out.

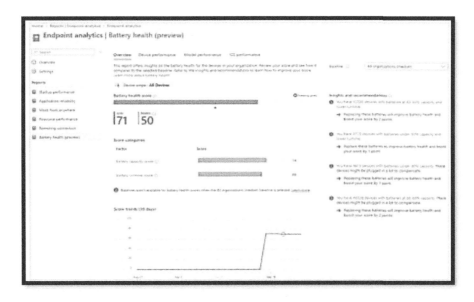

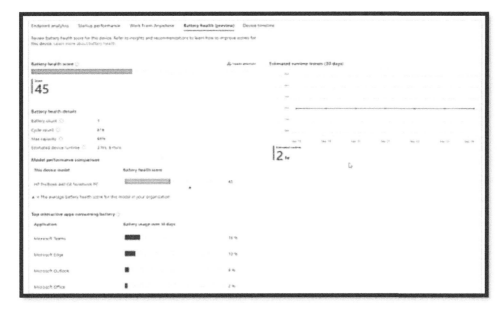

Enhanced Mobile Device Management

Microsoft Intune now has better mobile device control features that let businesses handle a lot of different devices more easily. You can easily apply security policies, set up device settings, and control devices directly from a central center with the newest features. All of your devices, like phones, tablets, and computers, can be managed with Microsoft Intune. This makes sure that your devices are safe and useful. In addition, Microsoft Intune's improved mobile device management features provide a wide range of tracking and feedback tools. With these more advanced features, you can learn a lot about how devices are used, spot possible security risks, and be ready for any problems that might happen.

Device Usage

You can learn about how devices are being used in your company by keeping track of how they are being used. This data can help you find any possible errors or places to make things better when it comes to allocating and using devices. Monitoring how a device is used can also help you find any strange or illegal activities, so you can stop them right away to lower any security risks. With Microsoft Intune's reporting tools, you can make thorough reports on how well devices and policies are being followed. You can find any devices that aren't up to date or in compliance with your organization's policies using these reports, which give a clear picture of the general security state of your devices. This lets you quickly fix any problems with not following the rules and make sure that all devices are always safe and up to date.

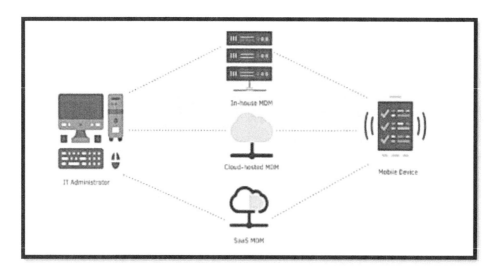

Improved Application Management

With Microsoft Intune's improved application management features, you can completely change how you handle apps in your business. You can make sure that your users can easily access the right apps at the right time by simplifying the release and download processes. That's because Microsoft Intune makes it easy to distribute and update apps, which saves you time and money. Microsoft Intune's better application management features give you a full set of tools to improve the performance and user experience of your apps. You can decide who can use certain apps and set limits based on user jobs if you have more control over application policies and rights. With this fine-grained level of control, you can customize the application environment to fit your company's specific needs and requirements, ensuring that only allowed users can access private apps and data. You can also use Microsoft Intune to apply strict data protection methods that keep your company's private information safe. To stop data leaks and illegal access, you can use encryption methods, policies to stop data loss, and safe access controls. With these strong security measures in place, you can rest easy knowing that your data and apps are safe from possible dangers.

Advanced Security Features

Every business puts security first, and Microsoft Intune has advanced security tools to keep your devices and data safe. You can use strong security measures like limited access policies, multi-factor login, and data protection with the most recent updates. When you combine Microsoft Intune with other Microsoft 365 security tools, you get a full security system to protect your company's assets. Microsoft Intune also has advanced security features that make it possible to find and respond to threats before they happen. You can use the power of machine learning to spot fishy behavior, find malware, and stop data breaches. You can stay one step ahead of possible dangers and give your devices and data the best level of protection with Microsoft Intune.

Streamlined Enrollment Process

The process of enrolling devices can take a long time and be hard to understand. But Microsoft Intune's streamlined features make the registration process easier, making it faster and easier to add devices to your company's management system. Microsoft Intune has an easy-to-use interface that makes registration quick and easy, no matter if the devices belong to the company or the user. Administrators and users can both save time during the training process with Microsoft Intune. By getting rid of the need to manually join devices, businesses can make sure that everything goes smoothly and quickly for everyone. The easier registration process in Microsoft Intune makes things easier for both managers and users. Users can quickly join their devices and get to work.

Self-Service Option

One of the best things about Microsoft Intune's simplified registration process is that it lets users do things on their own. Users can join their devices, download the necessary apps, and gain access to company resources without the need for expert support. By empowering users to handle their device management, this self-service method not only increases user output right away but also decreases dependency on IT help. By letting users join devices themselves, Microsoft Intune gets rid of the trouble and waits time that comes with manually enrolling devices. Users can sign up their devices whenever it's convenient for them, without having to wait for IT help. Because they can quickly set up their devices and begin using the apps and resources they need without any technical difficulties, this enables users to be more independent and productive.

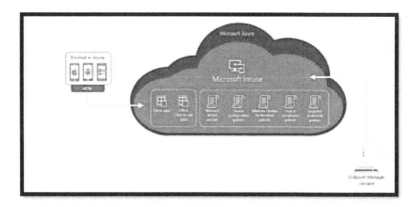

Seamless Integration with Microsoft 365

Microsoft Intune works with Microsoft 365 without any problems, making a single tool for managing devices and getting work done. The interface lets you make the most of Microsoft 365 services like Microsoft Teams, SharePoint, and OneDrive while maintaining ring security and compliance. You can give users a smooth experience across all devices and apps with Microsoft Intune. The connection with Microsoft 365 also makes it easier to work together and get things done. You can easily keep data safe and compliant while sharing papers, working together in real-time and accessing files from anywhere. Your company can accomplish more with ease thanks to Microsoft Intune, which brings together the power of device control and productivity tools.

Requirements for Microsoft Intune

Licensing requirements

You need to be given an Intune account to use Microsoft Intune. You can also get a sample ticket that lasts for 30 days so you can test the service and make sure it works. You don't need an Azure account to use Microsoft Intune as a service. You don't need an Azure account if you have Windows 365 + Entra ID Join. When you use the service with Hybrid Entra ID join, on the other hand, you'll need to set up an Azure virtual network, which means you'll need an Azure account.
The following types of licenses let you use Microsoft Intune:
- Intune-only license
- Microsoft 365 E3
- Microsoft E5
- **Enterprise Mobility + Security (EMS)** E5

There's a good chance that your company already has one of these licenses and can use Microsoft Intune. It's pretty simple to make a free account. Just go to https://admin.microsoft.com and click on **Billing**, then **Purchase Services**. Purchase the trial (for free) by looking for one of the titles mentioned above. You don't need a credit card or any other kind of payment information to do this.

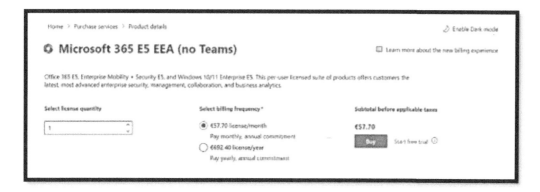

Supported OSes

- **For Microsoft:**
  - Windows 11 (Enterprise single- and multi-session versions)
  - Windows 10 (Enterprise single- and multi-session versions)
  - Windows 10 Pro Education
  - Windows 10 Enterprise 2019/2021 LTSC
  - Windows 10 IoT Enterprise (x86, x64)
  - Windows 10 Teams – Surface Hub
  - Windows Holographic for Business
- **Supported mobile OSes:**
  - **Apple:**
    - Apple iOS 15.0 and later
    - Apple iPadOS 15.0 and later
    - macOS X 11.0 and later
  - **Google:**
    - Android 8.0 and later (including Samsung Knox Standard 3.0 and higher)
    - Android Enterprise
    - Android open-source project device

Next, let's explore the web browser versions that support Microsoft Intune.

Required web browser versions

Depending on your specific IT admin tasks, you might use one of the following admin portals:

- Microsoft Intune admin portal
- Microsoft 365 admin portal
- Entra admin center

The following browsers are supported for these portals:

- Microsoft Edge (latest version)
- Safari (latest version – Mac only)

- Chrome (latest version)
- Firefox (latest version)

Now that we know about the OS and browser requirements, let's take a look at the hardware requirements for Windows 11.

Windows 11 hardware requirements

Windows 11 is now on its third release after **GA** (**General Availability**). However, there are some fundamental changes to the requirements of the hardware for Windows 11 compared to **Windows 10 that we would like to explain:**

- **Processor**: A 1 GHz or faster processor with at least two cores, compatible with 64-bit architecture or System on a Chip (SoC).
- **RAM**: A minimum of 4 GB of RAM.
- **Storage**: At least 64 GB of available storage space is required for Windows 11 installation. Additional storage may be needed for updates and certain features.
- **Graphics card**: The graphics card must be compatible with DirectX 12 or later and have a WDDM 2.0 driver.
- **System firmware**: UEFI firmware with Secure Boot capability.
- **TPM**: Trusted Platform Module (TPM) version 2.0 is required.
- **Display**: A high-definition (720p) display with a minimum size of 9 inches and support for 8 bits per color channel.
- **Internet connection**: An active internet connection is necessary for updates and certain functionalities.

There might be additional requirements over time for updates and to enable specific features within the OS. The requirements are important to follow as you might run into complications once you start upgrading to Windows 11:

In the image above, you can see screenshots of mistakes that are shown during the installation of Windows 11. Before you can start the in-place upgrade process, it checks to see what tools you need. Before you upgrade, you should also know about some other ways in which Windows 10 and 11 are different. **These are where you can find them:**

- **The following key deprecations and changes can be found in Windows 11's Start menu.**
  - Live tiles
  - Dynamic previews
  - Named groups and folders of apps
- Sites and apps that are pinned will not move when you upgrade from Windows 10.
- New, up-to-date Windows logos.
- The Windows Store app has been changed so that Win32 apps can now be installed.
- A brand-new tool that lets you use multiple windows and snap apps next to each other.
- You can no longer use live tiles. Check out the new widgets feature for material that can be seen at a glance and changes over time.
- Tablet mode has been taken away, and new features and functions have been added for attaching and detaching the keyboard.
- **The following things about how the taskbar works have changed:**
  - **People** are no longer on the taskbar.
  - The **system tray (systray)** may not show some items anymore, including ones that were customized in the past for newer devices.
  - You can only align to the bottom of the screen.
  - Apps can't change parts of the taskbar anymore.
  - Timeline has been taken away. Microsoft Edge has some similar features.
  - Internet Explorer has been taken away. Edge is the better alternative, and it has an IE mode that might come in handy sometimes.
  - The Math Input Panel has been taken away.
  - You can still use the Snipping Tool, but the Windows 10 version no longer has the old look and functions. Instead, it now has those of the app that used to be called Snip & Sketch.
  - Center alignment on the desktop.

In the next image, you can see how the new Windows 11 desktop looks and works:

Intune Administrator Licensing

By default, all Intune administrators need to have a Microsoft Intune license. At a later time, you can modify this in the Microsoft Intune admin center (https://intune.microsoft.com), which lets you grant admins access to Microsoft Intune without needing an Intune account.

If you want to get an administrator license, do the following:

1. Click on **Tenant Admin**, then on **Roles**, then on **Administrator Licensing**.
2. Click **Allow access to unlicensed admins**:

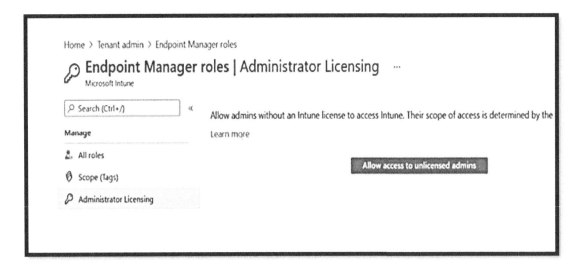

NOTE: Once this setting is made, it can't be changed back.

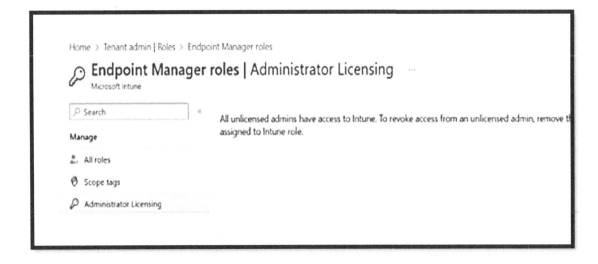

Go to https://admin.microsoft.com in the Microsoft 365 admin center. You can give your Intune license to someone else if you are a global administrator.

It comes with Microsoft 365 E3/E5, Microsoft 365 F1/F3 for Firstline Workers, and EMS E3. You can also use Microsoft Intune on its own. Microsoft Intune can be used with a lot of different licenses. Always talk to your license partner to make sure you have the right license for the situation. For a person in your client to add their device to Intune, they also need a license.

CHAPTER 2

GETTING STARTED WITH MICROSOFT INTUNE

Setting up Microsoft Intune

To successfully set up Microsoft Intune, follow the step-by-step guide, focusing on creating an Azure Portal account, accessing the Microsoft Intune portal, configuring Intune policies, enrolling devices, and managing apps and software updates. Each sub-section provides a solution to tackle a specific aspect of the setup process.

Creating an Azure Portal Account

To get Microsoft Intune up and going, make an Azure Portal account. To keep your company's devices, apps, and info safe, you need to do this. How to do it:

- Visit the Azure Portal page.
- Click "Create a Free Account".
- Fill in the information asked for.
- Use a code sent to your phone or email to verify who you are.

Take charge of managing your devices right now! Use all of Intune's features to make your business safer and more efficient.

Accessing the Microsoft Intune Portal

- Sign up to your Microsoft Office 365 account.
- Go to the **Admin Center**.
- Click "**Intune**" on the "**Admin centers**" tab.

You can get to the **Microsoft Intune Portal** by following these steps. It lets you control devices and apps with a lot of features and settings. Management of devices and apps, execution of security policies, and more! When it first came out in 2011, **Microsoft Intune** was called **"Windows Intune."** It has changed over the years to become a way to control devices and apps in the cloud.

Configuring Intune Policies

When you go to the Policy Configuration page, you'll see some choices. For device enrollment, app control, compliance settings, and more, these allow you to customize them. There are different ways that each strategy is meant to manage devices and protection. You can, for example, limit the installation of apps or make sure that only devices that you manage can access business resources. Just pick out the feature you want to change and follow the on-screen directions to set up a policy. You can pick settings like how long your password needs to be, how security works, and which websites and apps you can access. Before setting Intune policies, evaluate your organization's needs. Think about what kinds of devices your workers have and how they can get to private information. Use these things to help you make policies that are both safe and easy for users. Also, look over and change Intune's policies regularly. Keep up with the latest Microsoft Intune tools and best practices in your field. This will keep devices safe and give users a good experience.

Enrolling Devices in Intune

Signing up your devices for Microsoft Intune is a very quick and easy process. It lets you protect and control all of your devices from a single place. **Make sure your gadgets are safe by following these steps and following the rules set by your company.**

- **Get your devices ready:** Make sure they meet the requirements before adding them to Intune. One way to do this is to make sure they have an open online connection and are using a supported OS version.
- **Enroll your devices: Here's what you need to do to add a device to Intune:**
  o Open up the device and go to Settings.
  o Click "Add an account" after selecting "Access work or school."
  o Type in the email address that is linked to your Intune account. Follow the on-screen instructions.
- **Set up policies for devices:** Set up device policies to guarantee security and compliance once you're joined. Some of these policies could be setting rules for passwords, turning on encryption, or putting limits on apps. Change these settings so that they fit the needs of your business.

This is important to know: enrolling devices to Intune not only gives you more control over their safety, but it also makes admin jobs easier and increases productivity for both end users and IT managers. Don't miss the chance to use Microsoft Intune to make managing your devices easy. You can get better protection and follow your company's policies by signing up your devices right away. Now is the time to take charge of your device control journey!

Managing Apps and Software Updates

Identify App/Software Update Needs

- Make a list of all the apps and tools that need to be updated.
- Write down what each update needs to do, like fixing bugs and making the system more secure.

Create Update Deployment Rings

- Put devices into deployment rings based on things like the type of device or the roles of the user.
- Put app and program updates for each ring in order of how important they are.

Configure Intune Update Policies

- Go to the Microsoft Endpoint Manager Admin center.
- To set policies for app and software updates, go to "Devices" > "Update policies."
- Make policies fit the needs of your organization by letting automatic installations happen or setting up maintenance windows.

Unique Considerations

- Intune lets you plan phased deployments,
- This means slowly rolling out updates to different groups within a deployment ring.
- This helps find any problems before they affect a lot of people.

True History

In the past, it was hard to keep track of many apps and programs on many devices. It was hard work and took a lot of time to keep all systems up to date. But Microsoft Intune made it easier to handle app and software updates by giving you a single platform. It made working with IT easier. It continues to give businesses power over their app environment and the best protection and usefulness.

Troubleshooting Common Issues during Setup

Deal with authentication and permissions issues as well as device enrollment errors to fix common problems that happen during the setup of Microsoft Intune. If you look at these parts, you'll find ways to make sure that setting up Microsoft Intune goes smoothly.

Authentication and Permissions Issues

During setup, authentication and permissions are very important. They make sure that only people who are allowed to use an app or system and do things with it. But troubles with authentication and permissions can happen. If you're having trouble authenticating, check the login information again. Make sure that the username and password are right, as well as the form of the letters. Check to see if the account has enough permissions and if two-factor authentication is set up. Problems with permissions can also make settings take longer. Change or review the levels of access. Allow users and groups to do what they want, so they can get things done without any issues. This helps protect the environment. Challenges can come up in strange scenarios. To figure out what's going on, check to see if the parts work with each other, how the network is set up, and if any firewall settings could stop login or rights. Do not wait for a long time to start the setup process. Quickly fix any login and permissions issues by following the right steps. For help, you can look it up online, read the instructions, or call customer service. Users can use the systems or app's features and functions to resolve issues quickly. Don't let authentication and permissions get in the way of setting up. Get through any problems you face and use your new tools to their fullest!

Device Enrollment Errors

If you make a mistake while setting up your device, it can be very annoying. But don't give up! **These problems are easy to fix with this 3-step guide, and you can quickly activate your device.**

- Check the Internet connection. Make sure it stays put. Errors can happen if the connection is weak or unstable. You could try a different network or reset your Wi-Fi router's settings.
- Verify your credentials. Please make sure that the login and password are right. Authentication mistakes can happen when details are wrong. There may be typos or extra spaces, so check again.
- Update your device software. Errors can also happen with old software. Find any updates that are out there and install them before you try to join again.

If you want to solve the problem, follow these steps. Each mistake might have features that are unique to the person or the type of device. Help should be found through the proper support lines of the device's maker, or by reading their documentation. This info comes from some support groups and public documents made available by big tech companies like **Apple, Microsoft, and Google**. That's it! You now know how to fix mistakes that happen during setup for devices.

Signing up for Intune

Sign up for a Microsoft Intune free trial

For 30 days, you can try Intune for free. Sign in with an account you already have at work or school and add Intune to your contract. You can make a new account if you want to use Intune for your business.

Note: After making a new account, you can't join an old work or school account.

If you want to try Microsoft Intune for free, just follow these steps:

- Go to the page for setting up your Intune account.
- Type in your email address and click "Next."

When you sign up for the Intune trial, you can use an existing account or create a new one if you already have one set up with a different Microsoft service. The steps below are for making a new account.

- To create a new account, click **Set up account.**

- Put in your name, phone number, full company name, company size, and area. Look over the last few pieces of information and click Next.

- To make sure the phone number you added is correct, click Send verification code.

- On your mobile device, enter the verification code, and then click "Verify."

- Sign up for a free account with a username and domain name that fits your business or group. There will be **".onmicrosoft.com"** after your name. To see if it's available, click **"Save."** To go on, click Next. You can change this domain name to your name later if you want to.

- You'll see your user name after you create an account. This is the name you'll use to sign in to Intune. In addition, the email address you gave during the sign-up process receives a message with your account information. This email lets you know that your account is now active.

Note: Clicking "**Get Started**" will take you to the homepage of the Microsoft 365 admin center. It will take you to Your Goods where you can see information about your Microsoft Intune Trial subscription if you click Manage your subscription.

Sign in to Intune in the Microsoft Intune admin center

Follow these steps to sign in to the admin center if you haven't already:

1. Open a new browser tab and type **https://intune.microsoft.com** into the address bar.

2. To sign in, use the user ID you were given in the last step. Your user ID will look something like this: yourID@yourdomain.onmicrosoft.com.

You will also receive an email message containing your account information and the email address you gave during the sign-up process when you sign up for a trial. Your trial is now live, as this email shows. **Tip**: As a helpful hint, you might have better results with Microsoft Intune if you use a computer in normal mode instead of private mode.

Accessing the Intune dashboard

1. **Sidebar**
   - Home: This is the home page.
   - Dashboard: Status page that you can customize
   - All Services: A list of all services, including favorites that can be customized
   - Devices: This is a link to the panel for your devices, which has all of their features.
   - Apps: All apps used with Intune
   - Endpoint Security: Intune has settings for your devices that are specific to Endpoint Security.
   - Reports: These show the state of configurations, Windows updates, failed policies, and a lot more.
   - Users: You can directly access all users in Entra ID.
   - Groups: You can directly access all groups in Entra ID.
   - Tenant Administration: This is a link to intune relevant tenant settings.
2. Tenant name
3. Intune Status
4. Notifications and account options
5. Intune News and Customer Success
6. Documentations and Trainings

First Steps

- Add a domain to your Microsoft 365 tenant.
  - Intune could work without this step, but it would only use the backup domain (tenantname.onmicrosoft.com).
- Give out licenses using either dynamic or static Entra ID groups.
- Make a company logo in Entra ID and Intune
  - This is important for the setup screens on Autopilot devices and the Company Portal.

Understanding Intune terminology and concepts

Microsoft Intune is a full cloud-based service. It is part of Microsoft's Endpoint Management suite. In a current, mobile-centric setting, it focuses on controlling and protecting devices, apps, and data.

Before we get into Intune's terms and ideas, let's look at some of its most important parts:

1. **Enrollment**: This is the process of adding a device to Intune's control range. This could be a phone, tablet, or computer. Users can join devices directly or automatically using Device Enrollment Programs (DEP) for Apple devices, Android Enterprise for Android devices, or Windows Autopilot for Windows devices.
2. **Profiles**: Intune sets up settings and policies on devices that have been enrolled using profiles. These profiles can include app protection policies (for protecting business data within apps), device setup profiles (for settings like Wi-Fi, VPN, and email), and compliance policies (to make sure devices meet security standards).

3. **Apps**: Intune handles both company-owned apps and apps that you bring your own device (BYOD). It can set up and handle web apps, apps from the Microsoft Store, and line-of-business (LOB) apps that are specific to your company.
4. **Conditional Access**: This feature makes sure that only devices that are legal and have the right security settings (like having up-to-date software and encryption turned on) can access company resources like email or SharePoint Online. One important part of Intune's security features is its Conditional Access policies.
5. **Compliance**: Intune helps businesses make sure that devices follow legal guidelines. This means looking for things like OS version, device security, and the need for a PIN. Until they meet the requirements, devices that don't follow the rules can't access company data.
6. **Security Baselines**: These are sets of security settings that are already set up the way Microsoft recommends them to keep devices safe. You can quickly improve the security of your devices by applying these baselines through Intune.
7. **Inventory**: Intune gives you thorough information about the devices you handle that are in your inventory. This includes information about the hardware, apps that are installed, the state of compliance, and more. Monitoring the health of devices and making sure they are safe requires this info.
8. **Roles and Permissions**: Intune uses role-based access control (RBAC) to control who can do what. People with different jobs, such as Global Administrator, Intune Administrator, and Help Desk Operator, can access different Intune features and functions to different degrees.
9. **Reports**: Intune makes reports on things like security issues, app usage, device compliance, and more. These reports give you information about the health and safety of your device's surroundings as a whole.
10. **Integration**: Other Microsoft services, such as Azure Active Directory (AD), Microsoft Endpoint Configuration Manager (formerly SCCM), Azure Information Protection, and Microsoft Defender for Endpoint, work well with Intune. This lets you handle devices, keep them safe, and keep track of who you are all at the same time.

CHAPTER 3

ESTABLISHING ENROLLMENT FOR WINDOWS

How to Construct Update Rings

When you give fully controlled machines to users, you don't want them to update themselves without your control over when and what updates they get. Users also shouldn't choose to install secret builds on their own. You will need to set up some update rings if you don't have the Windows Enterprise license to use Autopatch or if you'd rather handle the updates yourself. You can tell Windows as a Service how and when to update your Windows 10 or 11 devices with quality and feature updates by setting up update rings. When you switch to Windows 10 or 11, the new features and quality updates include everything from the earlier updates. You can be sure that your Windows devices are up to date as long as you have the most recent fix loaded. You have to install the whole update now, not just a part of it like in older versions of Windows. Update rings can also be used to get Windows 11 on devices that are compatible with Windows 10. The setting titled Upgrade Windows 10 devices to Latest Windows 11 update by selecting it as Yes is used to accomplish this during the policy creation process. Devices run the most recent version of Windows 11 when you change to Windows 11 using update rings. Devices that haven't started the upgrade won't start it again if you later change the setting back to No, but devices that are already in the process of updating will keep going. **Devices that have already been upgraded will still have Windows 11.**

1. Click on **Devices**, then **Windows**, and then **Update Rings** for Windows 10 and later.
2. Go to the **Update Rings** for Windows 10 and later page and click on **Create profile.**
3. Give the Name and Description values that are informative. This is very important here so that you can tell them apart quickly.

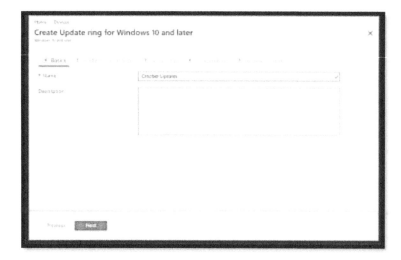

4. Under **"Update ring settings,"** change the settings to fit the needs of your business. Select Next after customizing the Update and User Experience settings. We need to set up our settings now. We'll look at each of these and the ideal setting for each ring because many of them will vary depending on your environment:

UI TIP

The choices start blue and change to purple when you configure them. The changes you make will not take away their purple color.

- o **Microsoft Product updates**: Windows Update is made possible by Microsoft Product Updates. This needs to be turned on.
- o **Windows drivers**: This lets Windows Update look for drivers and install them on the computer. If you'd rather use apps made by the seller for this, simply block here.
- o **Quality update deferral period**: You can choose how many days after Patch Tuesday quality updates will be installed by setting the quality update delay time.
- o **Feature update deferral period**: This value should be set to 0 for the feature update delay time so that we can use the feature update strategy. If the value is not 0, Intune will not pay attention to the extra policy.
- o **Upgrade Windows 10 devices to the latest Windows 11 release**: Support for Windows 10 will end in October 2025, so this is the best thing to do. But it depends on how ready you are to improve, so set it correctly.
- o **Set feature update uninstall period**: How many days after installing the update will you let people go back and undo the changes? For delayed installs, this is the number of days after the deferral period.
- o **Enable pre-release builds**: Your Pilot and Preview rings will need these.
- o **Automatic update behavior**: This is where you can choose when updates are downloaded and installed, as well as the hours when they are active. If you choose "Reset to default," the machine will figure out the busy hours and install itself accordingly. Set this to something that works for your business, like "7 a.m. to 7 p.m." for most office workers.
- o **Restart Checks**: This checks to see if the battery is more than 40% charged, if someone is at the computer, and if it's not in presentation mode, a full-screen app, the middle of a phone call, the middle of a game, or something else.
- o **Option to pause Windows updates**: You can do this from one place. At the user level, this takes place.
- o **Option to check for Windows updates**: Users are either allowed to check for updates or they are not.
- o **Use deadline settings**: This makes updates necessary, gives you time to do so, and lets updates happen automatically. Most of the time, it's best to leave this on so that you can make end-user devices reboot and stop them from putting it off over and over again, which could put the devices at risk.

5. If you want to use the tags on the update ring, go to Scope tags and pick + **Select Scope tags**. This will open the Select Tags box. To add tags to the update ring and return to the Scope tags page, select one or more tags and then click Select.

When you're ready, click **Next** to move on to Assignments.

Note: If the renter does not have any custom set scope tags, the Scope Tags configuration page might not show up when creating or changing some types of Intune policies. If you don't see the Scope Tag choice, make sure that at least one tag has been set up in addition to the default one.

6. Under **Assignments**, select **+ select groups to include** and then give them the update ring. To make the assignment just right, use **+ Select groups to exclude.** Select "Next" to go on.

Most of the time, we suggest sending update rings to groups of devices. Using device groups is in line with our advice for rolling out feature updates, and it gets rid of the need for a user to log in to a device before the policy can take effect.

7. Go to **Review + create** and look over the settings. When you're ready to save your Windows update ring, click **Create**. It shows up in the list of update rings as your new update ring.

Building feature updates

We need to keep an eye on the feature updates now that the update rings are set to 0 days. If **we don't, all of the computers will automatically upgrade to Windows 11 or any other new release every six months on the following Patch Tuesday:**

- Click on **Devices | Windows | Feature Updates for Windows 10 and later** in the Intune portal. Click **Create Profile.**

In general, you want all of your devices to be on the same version across the estate. However, if you have specific needs, you can create different profiles here and choose which devices to include or exclude. We will set devices to the most recent version of Windows 11, 22H2, for this case. Until we change the policy, this policy will bring all devices to Windows 11 22H2 and keep them there. The devices will stay on 22H2 when 23H2 comes out unless this policy is changed to reflect that:

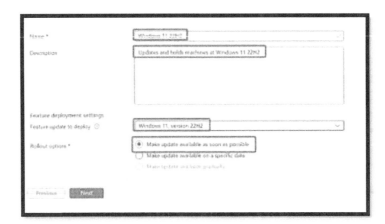

Keep in mind that the list of feature updates only includes operating system versions that are still supported. This means that if you have machines that are running anything older than Windows 10 21H1, they will automatically upgrade to the version you choose here. You can also choose which rollout methods to use to release more than one area at a time. If you want more control, you can also create different policies with specific times and focus your assignment groups. After you've changed these settings, click Next. Assign the policies to Autopilot Devices so that they can record everything in the estate. This will make everything match up. After that, click **Next**. Take a look at your policy again, and then click **Create**.

Customizing driver updates

You can also use Intune to get more precise control over driver updates for your devices. This way, you can choose whether to deploy them automatically or require approval before deployment. To check for any problems with the drivers before a full release, this will let you do it. Intune will check your estate immediately and add the drivers that are needed. You will need to share data with Microsoft again if you have decided not to do so for driver updates to show up.

- o In the beginning, go to **Devices** and then **Windows 10 and later updates.**
- o Create a new profile by selecting **Driver updates for Windows 10 and later.**
- o Type in a name and description for your profile, then click "Next."

Here is where you decide if updates should be accepted manually or done instantly. Note that after selecting this setting, you cannot change it; instead, you will need to delete the profile and create a new one. For better control, we are going to handle drivers manually in this case. When you're done, click Next.

- o If you choose Automatic, you will be asked to choose how many days drivers must wait before they can be accepted.
- o Since we're not setting any scope tags here, click Next.

For now, it's best to give to Device groups since policies for assignments are mostly based on devices. In this case, we are going to give Autopilot devices.

- o Make sure everything looks good, and then click "**Create**."

In the UI, we were able to create a driver update strategy. We can now look at how we automate things.

How to deploy Windows Autopatch with Microsoft Intune

As a Microsoft service, Windows Autopatch takes care of both quality updates and feature updates for Windows, Microsoft 365 Apps for Enterprise (also known as Office apps), Microsoft Edge browser, and Microsoft Teams. You don't have to worry about updates for approved goods once the service is turned on in your user and devices are successfully added. It will be taken care of by Microsoft.

Prerequisites of Windows Autopatch

- Windows 10/11 Enterprise E3 or higher licenses
- Azure AD P1 or higher licenses
- Microsoft Intune licenses
- Windows build 1809 or higher
- Users must exist in Azure AD (synced or cloud-only)
- Devices must be controlled by Microsoft Intune or Configuration Manager Co-managed by Microsoft

1. **Enable Windows Autopatch**

Go to the Microsoft Intune admin center for the next steps.

- Click on **Tenant Administration> Tenant enrollment** to get started. Select the box and click "**Agree**."

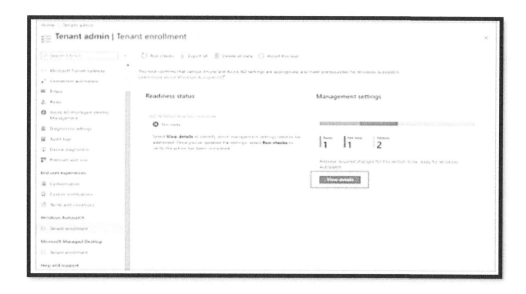

As a first step, we need to use the Readiness assessment tool to make sure we meet all the standards and can start the service. One of these states can be true for the test results.

- **Ready** means "ready to go"; nothing needs to be done.
- **Advisory**: This is just a suggestion for how to get the best experience once the service is up and running. It's not required, so it's not a problem.
- **Not ready**: Something that stops the show and needs to be fixed before you can go on.
- **Error**: This job can't be done because it doesn't have enough rights.

In my case, I have some suggestions that aren't ready points. Let's talk about them from the top to the bottom. Click on **View details**.

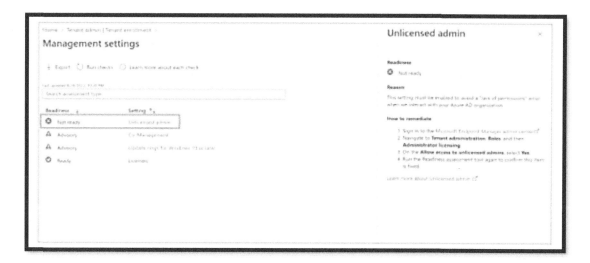

First, there's the matter of **unlicensed admin**. This is needed for the service, but I haven't turned it on yet. When you click on the setting on the left, the steps that need to be taken are shown on the right.

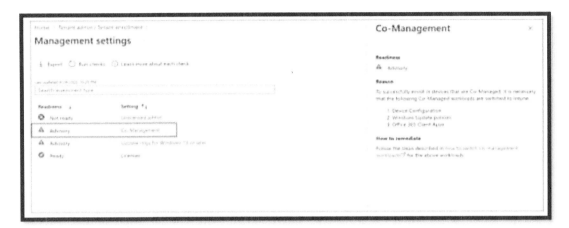

The second point is an advice about how to set up co-management. There is no co-management set up in my workspace, so I will ignore this one.

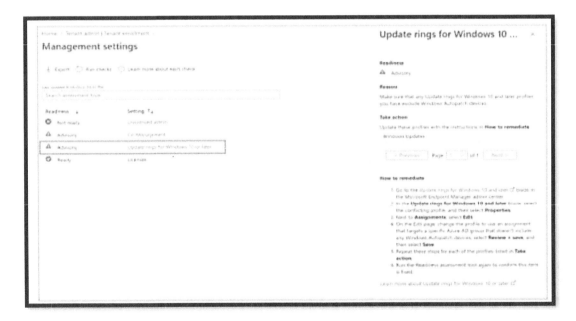

The next point is very important. I set up Update policies for devices that run Windows 10 or later. The settings for Windows Autopatch and these settings can clash. The current Windows Update rings policies should not apply to Autopatch devices. Make sure that this is not the case. For more information in the image, look at the steps on the right.

Once the settings have been changed as needed, click Run check.

We're now ready to go.

Click Enroll.

SELECT **I permit Microsoft to manage my Azure AD organization on my behalf** (if you do) and click "**Agree**." Type in the main admin contact information, then click "Next."

Press "Continue." The tools, such as security groups in Azure AD and policies in Microsoft Intune, will now be set up in the background.

The groups in the image above are formed in Azure AD when you deploy the Windows AutoPatch ring.

During the Windows AutoPatch deployment, the Configuration profiles for Windows devices are made. Along with these policies, Update rings for Windows 10 and later and Feature updates for Windows 10 and later are also made.

2. **Onboard devices to Windows Autopatch**

For devices to be added to Windows Autopatch, they need to be part of the Windows Autopatch Device Registration security group.

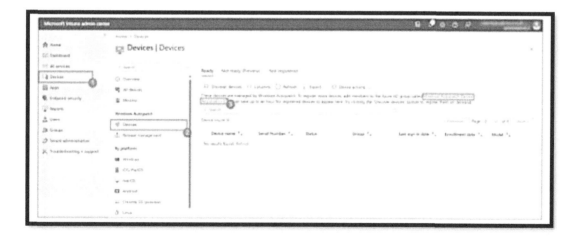

Go to **Devices** > **Windows Autopatch Devices** in the Microsoft Intune admin center. Click **Windows Autopatch Device Registration.**

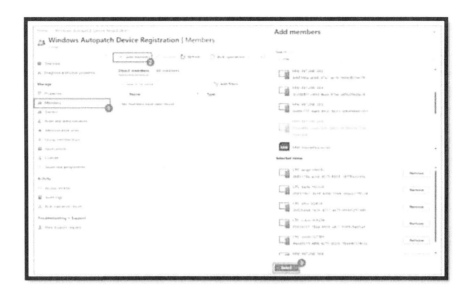

It will open the **Windows Autopatch Device Registration** security group in a new tab when you click on that link. To add the computer accounts, make sure the Members page is open and click "Add members." Go back to the **Microsoft Intune admin center** and click on **Discover devices**. When you connect the device to the Windows Autopatch service, you can see which ring it is given.

This can be one of the following rings.

- o **Test—Deployment** ring for testing updates before they are rolled out to production.
- o **First**-Early users
- o **Fast**—Quick rollout and use
- o **Broad**—The last ring for the broad rollout

You can change the update ring by going to **Device actions** > **Assign device group** after selecting a device.

3. **Managing Windows Autopatch**

In the Microsoft Intune admin center, I will briefly talk about where you can control Windows AutoPatch.

I added a **Windows Autopatch** section to the devices list after enrollment. You can see a list of **Ready** (onboarded) and **Not ready** devices on the **Devices** tab. Things that need to be done before a device can be a reason why it is not ready.

You can stop and start updates for each ring on the **Release Management tab**. Under the **Release Announcements** tab, you can also see what updates have been made public. You can choose to apply the **Expedited quality updates** and/or the **Microsoft 365 app updates** (which are turned on by default) in the **Release settings** tab.

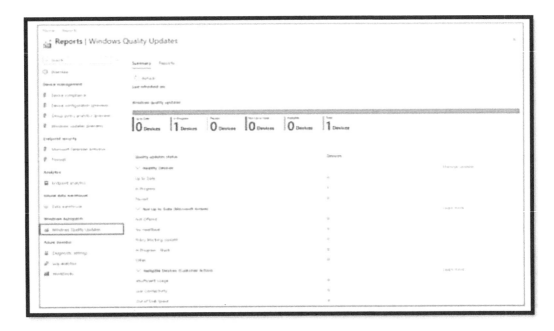

Under **Reports** in the Microsoft Intune admin center, you can now find a new section about Windows AutoPatch called **Windows Quality Updates**. You can see a list of all the device states here. This report may not be up to date for a few hours.

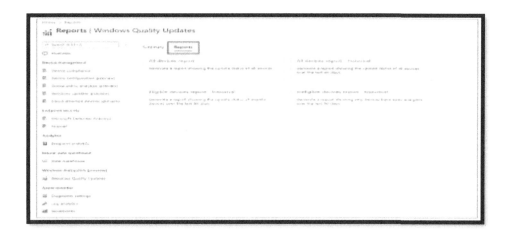

Reports can also show you how your surroundings have changed over time.

How to Arrange Windows Hello for Business

Windows Hello for Business (WHfB) lets you use a PIN, biometrics (like a fingerprint or face), or a FIDO2 security key for multi-factor authentication (MFA) on Windows devices. The Device Enrollment menu or the Settings library can be used to set this up at the tenant level or a more granular level. We will talk about both ways in this section. We will begin with the tenant level, which needs to be left at "**Not Configured**" for the Settings store to work.

Create a Windows Hello for Business policy

1. Go to the **Microsoft Intune admin center** and log in.
2. Select **Devices**, then **Enroll Devices**, then **Windows Enrollment,** and finally **Windows Hello for Business**. The pane for Windows Hello for Business appears.

3. **For Configure Windows Hello for Business, select one of the following:**
   - ○ **Enabled**. If you want to set up Windows Hello for Business settings, select this setting. When you choose "**Enabled**," you can see and change other Windows Hello settings for devices.
   - ○ **Disabled**. During device enrollment, choose this choice if you don't want to turn on Windows Hello for Business. Users cannot set up Windows Hello for Business when it is turned off. Even though this policy won't turn on Windows Hello for Business when it's set to Disabled, you can still change the settings below to make it work.
   - ○ **Not configured**. If you don't want Intune to manage the Windows Hello for Business settings, select this setting. Any Windows Hello for Business settings that are already in place on 10/11 devices are not changed. You can't change any of the other settings on the pane.

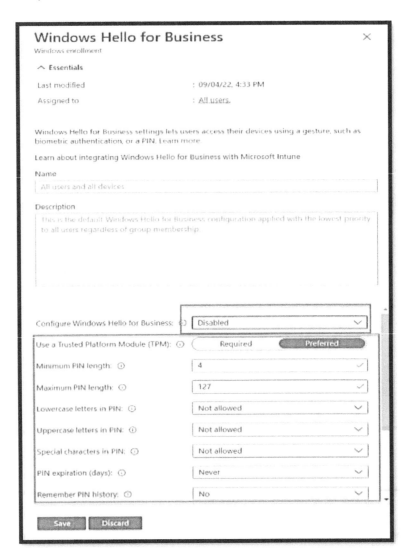

4. Set up the necessary settings that will be used on all registered Windows 10/11 devices if you chose "**Enabled**" in the previous step. Once these settings are set, click "**Save**."
   - **Use a TPM (Trusted Platform Module)**:

A TPM chip adds another level of security to data. Pick one of these numbers:
   - **Required** (default). Windows Hello for Business can only be set up on devices that have an accessible TPM.
   - **Preferred**. The devices try to use a TPM first. They can use software encryption if this choice is not available.
- **Minimum PIN length** and **Maximum PIN length**:

Sets devices to use the minimum and maximum PINs you choose to help make sure sign-in is safe. You can make sure that the PIN is at least four characters long, even though the usual number is six. The longest PIN that can be used is 127 characters.
- **Lowercase letters in PIN**, **Uppercase letters in PIN**, and **Special characters in PIN**.

Requiring capital letters, lowercase letters, and special characters in the PIN can make it tougher. Pick one from the following for each:
   - **Allowed**. People can use the character type in their PIN, but they don't have to.
   - **Required**. In their PIN, users must use at least one of the character types. For instance, it's usual to need at least one capital letter and one special character.
   - **Not allowed** (default). People shouldn't use these kinds of characters in their PIN. (This is also what happens if the setting isn't set.)

These are some special characters:! " # $% &'() * +, -. /: ; ^ = >? @ [\] ^ _'{ | } ^
- **PIN expiration (days)**:

It is a good idea to make sure that users change their PIN after a certain amount of time has passed. The default is 41 days.
- **Remember PIN history**:

Limits the use of PINs that have already been used. Most of the time, you can't use the last 5 PINs again.
- **Allow biometric authentication**:

This option lets you use a biometric login method, like a fingerprint or face recognition, instead of a PIN for Windows Hello for Business. Users still need to set up a PIN that will work in case biometric security doesn't work. Pick from:
   - **Yes**. Biometric authentication is possible with Windows Hello for Business.
   - **No**. All account types can't use biometric authentication with Windows Hello for Business.
- **Use enhanced anti-spoofing, when available**:

Sets whether the Windows Hello anti-spoofing tools are used on devices that can do so. For instance, finding a picture of a face instead of a real one.
When set to **Yes**, Windows makes all users use anti-spoofing for face features when it's possible to do so.
- **Allow phone sign-in**:

If this option is set to **Yes**, users can use a remote passport as a movable device to help them login to their desktop computer. The desktop computer needs to be linked to Microsoft Entra, and the other device needs to have a Windows Hello for Business PIN set up.

- **Enable enhanced sign-in security**:

Set up Windows Hello Enhanced Sign-in Security on devices that have the right hardware. What you can do:

- ○ **Default. Enhanced sign-in security will be enabled on systems with capable hardware.** Device users can't use third-party accessories to sign in to their device with Windows Hello.
- ○ **Enhanced sign-in security will be disabled on all systems.** To sign in to their device, device users can use additional devices that work with Windows Hello.
- **Use security keys for sign-in**:

This setting lets you remotely turn on and off Windows Hello Security Keys for all computers in a customer's business when it's set to "Enable."

Configuring at the group level

As you can see above, these settings are given immediately to all users, and there is no way to leave anyone out.

Instead, if this doesn't work in your system, you can change the general setup to "Not configured," which is what it will be set to by default if it hasn't been set up already:

- To do this, go to Devices, then Windows, Configuration profiles, click +Create, and then choose +New policy.
- Select **Windows 10 and later**, and then click **Create** after selecting **Settings Catalog**.
- Type in the values for Name and Description, and then click Next.
- First, click "Add settings." Then, scroll down until you see "Windows Hello for Business."

In this group, there are settings for both users and devices, so don't pick all of them. Choose any settings that work for your situation instead. You can choose the same settings here as you did at the tenant level, plus some extra features that are only available here, like better protection against face feature faking. You could also use the settings at the tenant level for most things and add to them with a settings catalog policy. Just be careful not to make too many changes at once.

- Once your settings are set, click **Next**:
- Click **Next** on the **Scope Tags page**.
- Assign as needed for your setting. To quickly create very similar policies, keep in mind that you can copy Settings catalog policies. After that, click **Next**.
- Look it over and click **"Create."**

Establishing Windows Autopilot Enrollment Profiles

We can now begin setting the policies so that we can ring enroll and supply devices now that we have our policies in place to handle them. It tells the device what to do when it hits the Autopilot service during the **Out of Box Experience (OOBE).** The first of these is the Windows Autopilot Enrollment Profile. With the Group Tag feature, you can generally give more than one name to a different Entra ID group. When you add devices to Autopilot, you can put them in the right Autopilot profile by using group tags. This lets you add devices to Dynamic Entra ID groups. Here are some reasons why you might want more than one profile:

- **Kiosk devices (using self-deploying mode):** For kiosk devices that are in self-deploying mode, these profiles are automatically set up and don't need any help from the user during setup. This means that a local device account can be set up to automatically sign them in. The policies can then be set up to make them run in a single app mode, which is typically a web browser.
- **International organizations:** The operating system language is chosen during Autopilot setup for international companies. You could use group tags to give a different identity based on the language needed.

How to do it...

To show this, we will set up a standard user-driven deployment. To set up and change things as needed for your environment, follow these steps:

- Go to **Devices** and then to **Enrollment**. Click on **Deployment profiles** after selecting **Windows**.
- Click on **Create profile**, and then pick **Windows PC**.
- Give the page a name and a description. You can also choose to turn all of the devices you've chosen into autopilot. If you apply this profile to an Entra ID group that has devices that aren't registered or supplied through Autopilot, the devices will be immediately added to the service, and any future restarts will also go through Autopilot during **OOBE**.
- Although we are only interested in Autopilot devices in this case, setting it to **Yes** is still safe. After that, click **Next**.
- On the next screen, we can set the basic OOBE settings, such as the language and what the users see when setting up their devices.
- Because of this, your deployment mode needs to be user-driven, which means that the user logs in during OOBE and sets things up as needed. Self-driven is used for kiosks and other devices that don't have a set customer.
- Leave "**Microsoft Entra joined**" as the value for "**Join to Microsoft Entra ID as.**" You can use hybrid join, but it doesn't work well with Autopilot, so you should try to avoid it if you can. Try not to bring any technical debt with you since we are setting up a whole new tenant and workplace.

- Setting the User account type to Standard is always the best thing to do. You don't have to give administrative rights, but you can use the **Entra ID role**, **Windows LAPS**, or **Endpoint Privilege Management** instead.

Allow pre-provisioned deployment (this used to be called "**White Glove**"). This is where an IT administrator can press the Windows key five times during OOBE to set up all the policies and apps that are specific to the device. The user only needs to go through the steps for user registration. With a big rollout or users on slow lines, this can be helpful, but you should also think about how quickly your environment changes. If your apps get updates often, users may get devices with apps that are out of date if the devices were pre-provisioned too far in advance. The serial number of the device (**or%SERIAL%)** is also configured in a ring template for device names. Since the name of the device is not as important with Intune as it used to be, this is not very important.

- Once the settings are set up the way they need to be for your area, click Next.
- Now we want to add this to the group of Autopilot devices. This group is set to add devices as soon as they are signed up for the Autopilot service, which means they can pick them up faster. Click Next after adding the group.
- The last step is to look over your settings and click **Create**.

Setting up an ESP (Enterprise State Roaming)

Setting up our ESP is the last thing we need to do before we can use Autopilot to deploy a Windows device. This is the screen users see after entering their passwords during OOBE. It shows them how their device is being set up and how they are progressing with onboarding.

Here are the steps to follow:

1. Go to **Devices** first, and then click on **Enrollment**. Select **Enrollment Status Page** from the **Windows** menu.

You can set up more than one page, and they will be asked based on their importance and then for group registration. The ESP is used to prevent a device from being used until a certain set of applications has been installed. You may need more than one if different departments, areas, or groups need to install key applications before they can log in and use the computers. Note that you cannot delete the Default page here, and while you can edit it, we will instead create a new one. We have added the Microsoft To-Do store application to show setting an ESP since we have yet to deploy any apps into this system.

2. Press the "**Create**" button.
3. Type in numbers for Name and Description, then click **Next**.
4. We need to tell Intune to show an ESP now. Now, change the setting for **Show app** and **profile configuration progress** to "**Yes**."

If you do this, the other settings will show up:

- ○ **Show an error when installation takes longer than the specified number of minutes**: When you deploy this setting, you should think about the apps that are being deployed and the fastest internet connection that your users might be using. If you set this too high and then mess up an app or script, the ESP will stay on the screen until the timeout is met, even though nothing will happen until the mistake is fixed. This is not a good way for users to interact. In the same way, if you set the number too low and your application is very big or complicated, the ESP might time out before the setup is finished as planned. Most of the time, 60 to 120 minutes is enough.

- ○ **Show custom message when time limit or error occurs**: If you have a helpline or a specific number for users to call when setting a new device, enter it here along with some directions for them. This will show a unique message when the time limit or mistake happens. This is the message that will be shown if Autopilot fails or runs out of time.

- ○ **Turn on log collection and diagnostics page for end users**: This will help you figure out what's wrong. In case a machine fails, users will see a button that lets them get the logs from the device itself. No one will be able to see it before then.

- ○ **Only show page to devices provisioned by out-of-box experience (OOBE):** If you want to only show the page on devices that were set up by out-of-box experience (OOBE), you should set this to "No." Setting this to "Yes" will show the ESP the first time someone logs in to an account that isn't the main user after the machine has been provisioned. When your IT team logs into a machine to fix something, they will not thank you for turning this off.

- ○ **Block device use until all apps and profiles are installed**: This turns the next three settings on or off. It will not be possible to block until apps are launched if you set it to "No."

- ○ **Allow users to reset device if installation occurs**: If Autopilot fails, you can either reset the device, let users continue using it, or do nothing. This is the first choice; it will show a "Reset" button that you can click to try provisioning again.

- ○ **Allow users to use a device if installation error occurs**: This is the second choice. If you set it to Yes, you will see a button that says "Continue" and it will take users to their screen if it doesn't work. The third choice is to set both to "No."

- ○ **Block device use until required apps are installed if they are assigned to the user/device**: If you set this to All, users will not be able to log in until all required apps are installed on all users' devices or devices in any groups that the user or group is a part of. Block device use until required apps are installed if they are given to the user or group. If you set this to "Selected," you can choose from the apps that have already been launched. We're going to use **Microsoft To-Do** for this case, as we already said.

- ○ One more choice is to only block apps that fail during the technician process. This is used with pre-provisioning and makes sure that your chosen apps are installed on a device when the user enrolls it. But during pre-provisioning, it downloads all the apps that are needed instead.

5. After you've changed the settings, click Next.

One ESP can be delivered to all users or devices if that's all you ever need. For this example, we will deploy to our Intune users group. This way, if you want to add more than one ESP setup for different user groups in the future, you will have more choices.

6. Click Next once you've chosen your deployment group.
7. Click Next to proceed to the Scope Tags page.
8. Last, make sure everything looks good, then click Create.

How to Enroll a Windows device

The first step in managing devices with Microsoft Intune is always the same: enrolling the device. As part of the enrollment process, Intune has to put a mobile device management (MDM) certificate on the device. This lets Intune talk to the device directly. IT admins can deploy policies, handle Intune, and carry out general management tasks on devices like Windows PCs through this communication with Intune.

What are the options for enrolling Windows devices?

IT departments can join Windows devices with Intune in some different ways. The main difference between these choices is usually who owns the device. There are different ways to join personally-owned devices and corporate-owned devices.

This is done so that personally-owned devices stay personal and corporate-owned devices stay corporate.

- **Windows Autopilot.** Windows Autopilot is the most popular choice for devices owned by businesses. Windows Autopilot is a service that utilizes a group of technologies to make setting up and deploying new devices easier. The device will automatically be linked to Microsoft Entra ID and signed up for Microsoft Intune during this process. The device is ready to be managed and used after that process is done.
- **Microsoft Entra join with automatic enrollment.** When IT managers can't use Windows Autopilot, they can set company-owned devices to automatically sign up for Microsoft Intune. During the out-of-box experience (OOBE), they can choose to connect the device to Microsoft Entra ID and give a work or school account. During that process, registration will happen in the same way that it did with Windows Autopilot. This method gives you less control over the whole span of the device, though, and it's not as easy to use.
- **Bulk enrollment with provisioning package.** When IT needs to enroll a lot of company-owned devices, bulk enrollment with a delivery package can be a faster option than Autopilot. During the OOBE, administrators can install a setup package that makes sure the device is immediately signed up for Microsoft Intune and joined to Microsoft Entra ID.
- **Intune Company Portal app.** The most popular choice for personally-owned devices is the Intune Company Portal app. If a person wants to add a device to Microsoft Intune, they can get the Intune Company Portal app from the Microsoft Store and follow the steps in

the app. Once this is done, the device is registered as a personal device, giving IT only a few control tools and information to work with.

- **Connecting a work or school account.** On devices that you own yourself, you can also add a work or school account using the steps in the Settings app. The result will be like the Intune Company Portal app, but it won't give you as much information about the device's state and won't give you a clear view of all the available apps.

What is the most common scenario for corporate-owned Windows devices?

Most of the time, Windows devices are added to Microsoft Intune by using Windows Autopilot to join devices that belong to a business. In this case, those devices must be linked to the Windows Autopilot service. By planning that during the purchase of those devices, you can accomplish this in the simplest way possible. When purchasing new devices, the majority of sellers and OEMs allow enrollment. Most of the time, this means that the seller gets access to the tenant's devices so that they can easily send the necessary data. The IT administrator has to upload the CSV file with the device details to the Windows Autopilot service if the seller only gives it to them.

What are the requirements for using Windows Autopilot?

Before an IT admin can use Windows Autopilot, there aren't many prerequisites that need to be met. **They need to make sure that the following rights and settings are in place:**

- At least a Microsoft Entra ID P1 license for quick enrollment and at least a Microsoft Intune P1 license for managing Intune. Both must have been given to users by IT.
- Setting up a basic Intune tenant and giving Microsoft Intune MDM power.
- Devices that have at least a version of Windows 10 or 11 Pro, Windows 10 or 11 Enterprise, or Windows 10 or 11 Education that is enabled.
- A Microsoft Account that is an administrator and has at least the Global Administrator or Intune Service Administrator job given to it.

How to set up automatic enrollment for Windows Autopilot via Intune

There are a few things that administrators need to do before they can use Windows Autopilot to automatically add devices to Microsoft Intune.

Configure automatic enrollment

Setting up automatic enrollment is the first thing that needs to be done. Once the device joins Microsoft Entra ID, automatic enrollment will make sure that it is immediately signed up for Microsoft Intune.

1. Go to **Devices** > **Windows** > **Windows enrollment** > **General** > **Automatic enrollment** in the Microsoft Intune admin center portal.
2. Click on one of the following choices on the Configure page to set up the MDM user scope (Image below).
   - **None.** Automatic enrollment in MDM is turned off.
   - **Some.** Only the chosen group can use MDM's automatic enrollment feature.
   - **All.** All users can have MDM automatic enrollment enabled.
3. Leave the MDM terms of use URL, MDM discovery URL, and MDM compliance URL as they are, and then click **Save** to save the changes.

Register the devices with Windows Autopilot

The second step is to add devices to Windows Autopilot. This step is only needed if the devices haven't already been added by the seller. This will use data that can be found in a CSV file.

1. Navigate to **Devices** > **Windows** > **Windows enrollment** > **Windows Autopilot Deployment Program** > **Devices** in the Microsoft Intune admin center portal.
2. Look at the image below to see the Windows Autopilot devices page. On that page, click **Import**. Click **Import** again after selecting the CSV file.

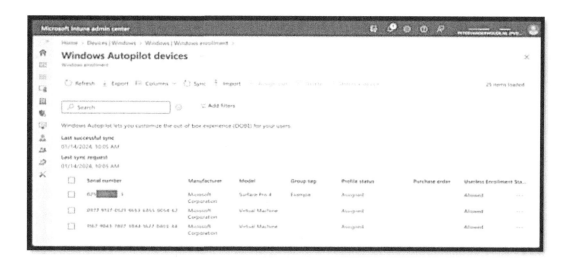

IT administrators can filter and group devices using the Windows Autopilot admin screen, which also offers views with crucial information. The Group tag is the most important of these, and IT can easily change it. **Use the following example code to create an Entra device group based on that tag:**

device.devicePhysicalIds -any (_ -eq "[OrderID]:Example"))

Create a Windows Autopilot deployment profile

The third step is to create a Windows Autopilot deployment profile, set the deployment mode of the devices, and modify the user's OOBE.

The following steps will show you how to make that profile:

1. To find Deployment Profiles, open the Microsoft Intune admin center portal and go to **Devices** > **Windows** > **Windows enrollment** > **Windows Autopilot Deployment Program.**
2. When you get to the page for Windows Autopilot deployment profiles, click **Create profile** and then pick **Windows PC**.
3. Give the user a name on the Basics page and click **Next**.
4. Set up at least the first two settings on the Out-of-box experience (OOBE) page, then hit Next (Image below).
   - ○ **Deployment mode.** Select **User-Driven** for a standard Windows Autopilot deployment. During enrollment, users give their passwords and the device is given to that user.
   - ○ **Join to Microsoft Entra ID as.** For the Microsoft suggested location to join new devices, select **Microsoft Entra joined**.

- o Based on internal policies, pick the settings that apply to the rest of them. Choose the account type, set the language, choose the name standard, and decide which pages should be shown.
5. Click **Next** to proceed to the Scope Tags page.
6. Set up the right assignment for the user based on an Entra device group on the Assignments page. You might want to use a group that is built on a Group tag.
7. Look over the settings on the Review + create page, then click **Create**.

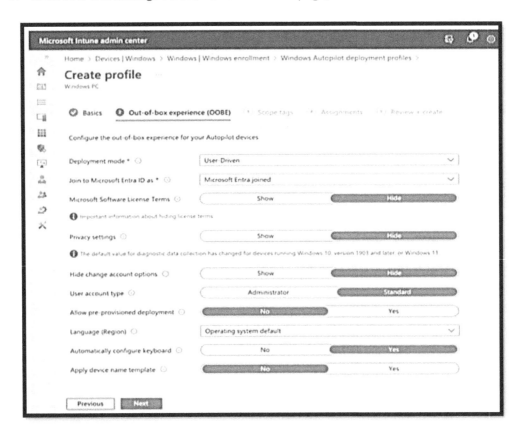

IT administrators can use Windows Autopilot to deploy company-owned devices once these settings are full and in place. Admins should also set up an Enrollment Status Page that will block the device until all of the necessary settings have been made and the necessary apps have been loaded. Don't forget to make changes to the setup options that will be used and the apps that need to be launched.

CHAPTER 4

SAFEGUARDING WINDOWS DEVICES

You can set up and deploy different Microsoft Intune security baseline profiles to different groups of Windows Intune and users to help protect your group and Windows devices. Each product's baseline is a group of preset settings that reflect the security stance that the product's security team has suggested. To set up devices with the settings that your company needs, you can deploy a basic baseline (unmodified) or modify your profiles.

Building a security baseline

Overview of security baselines

When you create a security baseline profile in Intune, you're making a template with many device configuration settings. Only the most current version of a security baseline can be used to create a new copy of that baseline when there are multiple copies available. You can keep using older baseline versions that you made before and change the groups they are given to. However, old versions don't let you change how their settings are set up. Create new baselines using the newest baseline version instead, or update older baselines to the newest version if you need to add new setting combinations.

As soon as possible, you should update older basic versions to the most recent version.
- New settings that weren't available in past versions can be added.
- Leave old settings behind and get rid of them if they're no longer needed.
- Make sure that the initial settings are in line with the latest security advice for the product in question.

Some common tasks to do when working with security baselines are:
- **Make a new profile instance;** set up the settings you want to use and give the baseline to groups.
- **Update an older baseline version with the most recent baseline version**. Have a character change the baseline version that is being used.
- **Take away an assignment to a baseline.** Find out what happens when you stop using a security baseline to manage settings.

Prerequisites

- For deploying security baselines with Intune, you need a Microsoft Intune Plan 1 subscription.

Tip: Intune can be used to set up and deploy security baselines with ease, but it does not create or describe the baselines itself. To deploy security baselines, there are other tools besides Intune.

- If you use baselines through Intune, you need to have a subscription to the controlled product that is currently live. Just because you use the Microsoft Defender for Endpoint standard doesn't mean you can use Microsoft Defender. Instead, the standard gives you a way to set up and control settings on devices that are licensed for and controlled by Microsoft Defender for Endpoint.
- If you want to handle baselines in Intune, you need to have the Policy and Profile Manager Job built into your account.

Create a profile for a security baseline

1. Go to the **Microsoft Intune admin center** and log in.
2. Select **Endpoint security** > **Security baselines** to see the list of available baselines.

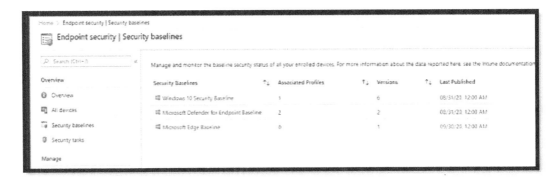

3. Select the baseline you want to use, and then click **Create Profile**.
4. **Set the following settings on the Basics tab:**
   - **Name:** Give your security baseline identity a name. Type in *Standard profile for Defender for Endpoint* as an example.
   - **Description**: Enter some text that tells what this baseline does for the description field. You can write anything you want in the description. You don't have to, but it's suggested.

To move to the next tab, select Next. Once you're in a new tab, you can click on the tab name to go back to a tab you've already seen.

5. On the tab for Configuration settings, look at the groups of settings that are available in the standard you chose. When you click on a group, you can see its settings as well as the default numbers for those settings. To find specific settings, do the following:
   - Select a group to see all the settings in that group.
   - There are details for a setting next to a light bulb icon. Setting details gives trust in setups by giving information about what other organizations have done successfully. You can get insights for some settings but not all of them.
   - In the search bar, types in terms that will narrow the view to only show the groups that meet your criteria.

For each baseline version, there is a default way to set up each setting. Change the settings so they work better for your business. Based on the purpose of the baseline, the same setting may be in more than one baseline, but the setting may have a different initial value in each baseline.

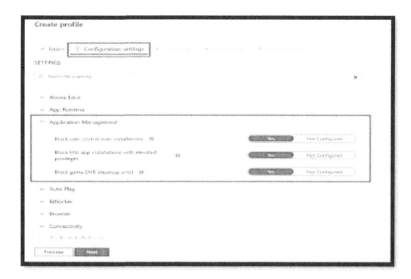

6. Click on the **Scope Tags** tab and then click on **Select Scope Tags**. This will open the Select tags pane where you can add scope tags to the profile.
7. Go to the **Assignments** tab and choose **"Select groups to include."** Next, give the baseline to one or more groups. Feel free to use **Select groups to exclude** to make the assignment just right.

Note: This is important to remember that security baselines need to be given to either user groups or device groups, depending on what settings are being used. This means that when assigning settings for both users and devices, you might need more than one standard.

Go to the Review + create tab and look over the details of the standard when you're ready to deploy it. To save and deploy the profile, select **Create**. When you create a profile, Intune sends it to the assigned group right away, where it is used.

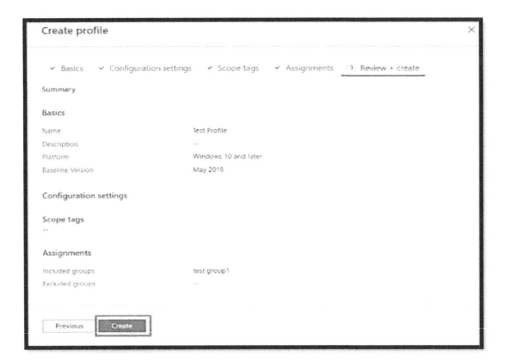

8. After you create a profile, you can change it by going to **Endpoint security > Security baselines,** picking the type of baseline you set up, and then choosing **Profiles**. Select the name you want from the list, and then go to **Properties**. Changes can be made to settings on any of the setup tabs. To save your changes, select **Review + Save**.

Change the baseline version for a profile

Before you change the version of a profile that is given to a group, test the change on a copy of the profile.

This way, you can make sure that the new baseline settings work on a test group of devices.

1. Go to the Microsoft Intune admin center and log in.
2. Select **Endpoint security > Security baselines**, then click on the tile for the baseline type with the profile you want to change.
3. Go to **Profiles** and check the box next to the profile you want to change. Then, go to **Change Version**.

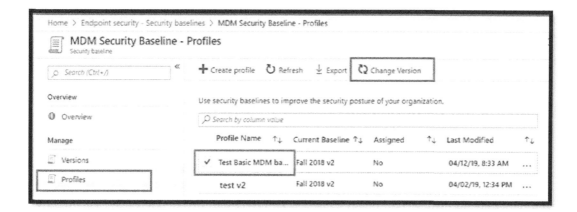

4. In the **Change Version box**, use the dropdown menu next to "**Select a security baseline to update to**" to choose the version instance you want to use.

5. Select **Review Update** to get a CSV file that shows the change between the current version of the profile's instance and the new version you chose. Go through this file again to see what settings have been added or taken away, as well as what their default numbers are in the new profile.
- Move on to the next step when you're ready.
6. Pick one of the two choices for **Select a method to update the profile**:
- **Accept baseline changes but keep my existing setting customizations:** This choice brings the changes you made to the baseline profile over to the new version you've chosen to use.

- **Accept baseline changes and discard existing setting customization options** deletes everything from your original profile. All of the settings in the new profile are set to their default values.
7. Select **Submit**. The baseline is deployed to the given group as soon as the change is finished, and the profile updates to the chosen baseline version.

Remove a security baseline assignment

If the settings in a security baseline are set to "Not configured" or a setting in a baseline no longer applies to a device, the settings on that device might not go back to a pre managed state. This depends on the settings in the security baseline. The settings are based on CSPs, and the change reduction can be done in different ways by each CSP. A new or different security baseline, a device configuration profile, Group Policy setups, or a direct edit of the settings on the device are additional steps that might later change settings on the device.

Duplicate a security baseline

You can create additional copies of your security baselines. When you want to give a group of devices a similar but separate baseline, it can be helpful to make a copy of the baseline. You don't have to rebuild the whole baseline manually if you make a copy. You can instead make a copy of any of your present baselines and then only make the changes that the new instance needs. You might only be able to change one setting and the group that the standard is given to. Give the copy a different name when you create a duplicate. The copy has the same scope tags and setting sets as the original, but it doesn't have any assignments. To add assignments, you need to change the new standard. Making a duplicate is supported by all security baselines. Once you've copied a baseline, you can change its settings by going back and editing the new copy.

To duplicate a baseline

1. Go to the Microsoft Intune admin center and log in.
2. Go to **Endpoint security** > **Security baselines** and pick the type of baseline you want to copy. Next, click on **Profiles**.
3. Right-click on the profile you want to duplicate and choose "**Duplicate**." You can also click on the ellipsis "..." icon to the right of the baseline and choose "**Duplicate**."
4. Give the baseline a new name, and then click "**Save**."

The new default profile shows up in the admin center after a Refresh.

To edit a baseline

1. Select the baseline first, and then click **Properties**.
2. To change the description, you can choose **Edit** for the following lists from this view:
   o Basics
   o Assignments

o   Scope tags
o   Configuration settings

You can **Edit** a profile's **Configuration settings** only when that profile uses the most recent version of that security baseline. For profiles that use older versions, you can open **Settings** to see how the profile's settings are set up, but you can't change them. You can change a profile's settings after it has been changed to the most recent baseline version.

3. When you're done making changes, click "**Save**" to keep them. You have to save changes to one category first before you can make changes to other categories.

Configuring an antivirus policy

- For the policy type, use the dropdown menu to choose **Microsoft Defender Antivirus.**
- Give the policy a **name and a description.**
- Change the settings so they work with your environment. If you're not sure about any of them, the small letter (i) in a circle next to each field will tell you more. After you've set up your settings, click Next.
- On the **Scope Tags page**, click **Next**.
- Assign the policy to your **Autopilot Devices** group once you're done setting up your settings.
- Click the arrow next to Defender to see all of your settings, then click **Create**.

Now, you've made your policy.

How to Fine-tune Windows Security Settings

We will now set up the Windows Security Experience policy to change how users feel when they look at Windows' security settings:

- Select **Windows Security Experience** from the Antivirus menu in Endpoint Security to create a new policy.
- Type in a **name and description** for the policy, then click "**Next**."
- Most of these are up to you, but make sure you turn on **Tamper Protection** at the very bottom. Turn off Family UI since this is a corporate machine. After that, change anything about your surroundings that needs to be changed.
- Press the **Next** button.
- Assign the policy to **Autopilot Devices**.
- Look it over, and then click Create.

How to configure your BitLocker preferences

- Select Disk encryption and create a strategy in Endpoint security.
- Choose a name and description for the policy, and then click Next.
- Change the Base Settings to match what you see in the image below:

- Make changes to the Fixed Drive Settings based on the image below:

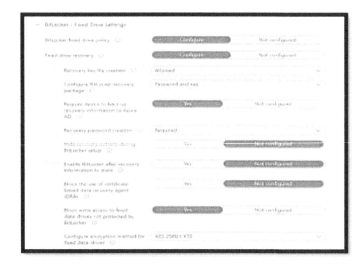

The only setting that needs to be changed in **OS Drive Settings** is the encryption method, but you might want to change **Startup authentication required** to **Yes** if you want to meet CIS compliance:

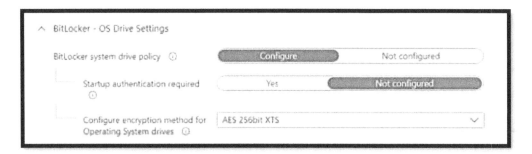

Removable Drive Settings are for your USB sticks. When you block completely, this setting is less important, but you should still do it just to be safe. **These are the times when we use CBC encryption instead of XTS:**

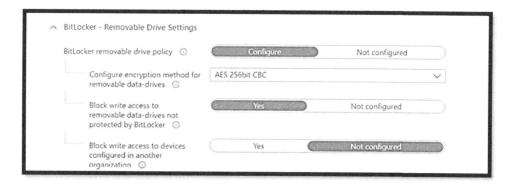

- Press the Next button.
- Now, click Next after assigning it to Autopilot Devices.
- Give the settings one last look and click Create.

Personalizing Windows Firewall

The Reusable settings choice will be shown to us when we look at Windows Firewall. To allow a piece of software to run or to further limit a selection of devices, an environment will frequently have multiple firewall policies for various user and group groups. With Reusable Settings, you can set up your own firewall rules once and then use them across policies without having to add them manually every time.

Just to give you an idea, this rule would block all Google domains:

After learning about Removable Drive Settings, follow these steps to set up the default Microsoft Defender firewall policy:

1. Go to the Microsoft Intune admin center and log in.
2. Click on **Endpoint Security** > **Firewall** > **Create policy** > **Windows 10, Windows 11, and Windows Server** > **Windows Firewall** > **Create**
3. Type in a name and, if you want, a description > **Next**

4. In the **configuration settings**, set the following for each type of network site (Domain, Private, and Public):
   - **Log file path**
   - **Enable log dropped packets**
   - **Enable log success connections**
   - **Log max file size**
5. Select **Next** > **Next**
6. Put the policy in a group that has the devices or users you want to set up as members > **Next** > **Create**.

Executing ASR regulations

Bad actors often go after the more well-known and well-documented weak spots in a standard machine build. Examples include Adobe Acrobat Reader, Office Macros, and Java Script. Luckily; there are built-in ASR rules that can be turned on to stop these from happening. There is also the choice to turn them on in Audit mode if you are worried about how they might affect your application.

- To set these up, go to the Endpoint security blade; click Attack surface reduction, and then select **Create** a new policy.
- Select Attack surface reduction from the list.

Again, you will notice that we have reusable settings here; this is where you can set the USB and printer device IDs. These have nothing to do with ASR rules, but they do have something to do with other policies that can be set up in this blade.

The steps below will show you how to make a new ASR policy:

- Give your policy **a name and a description**, and then click **Next**.
- On the **Settings** screen, look over each policy and think about how it might affect your environment. If you're not sure or think it might, it's better to be safe than sorry and set it to Audit mode at first.
- Then look at the reports, and turn it on if it doesn't show any problems. It's safer to have enabled, but the tools still need to work for the users and apps.
- Here, we're setting everything to **Block** because this is a lab situation and there aren't any legacy apps to worry about.
- **ASR Only per Rule Exclusions** will show up when you change a setting. This can make the policy setting not apply to a certain application (type in the application executable).
- As with other policies, choosing the letter "i" inside a circle will show you what the policy does. If you're still not sure, use **Audit or Warn**.
- You can set up your policy settings and then click **Next**.
- Click Next once more on the Scope Tags page.

- Choose whether to give to users or devices on the **Assignment** screen based on how your user profiles look. For instance, if your finance department uses an Office add-in, you might want a slightly less strict policy just for them. You don't want to have to loosen it for everyone in the company.
- Then, as normal, review your policy and click **Create** to make it official.

Enrolling in Defender for Endpoint

- Click **Settings**.
- Next, click on **Endpoints**.
- Now, scroll to the bottom of the page. You should see a setting called **Microsoft Intune Connection**. Slide that to **On**.
- After that, click **Save Preferences** and go back to the Intune portal.
- Go to **Endpoint Security**, then **Endpoint detection and response**, and then create a new policy **(Windows 10, Windows 11, and Windows Server)**.
- Choose **a name and a description** for the policy.
- Now that the Intune **Connector within Security Centre** is turned on, we can choose the **"Auto from connector"** choice from the dropdown menu for the **Microsoft Defender for Endpoint client configuration package type**. If it's not there, make sure that the Intune Connector was turned on and saved properly in the **Security Portal** steps before.
- Click **Next** after setting up your sample share.
- Click **Next** to proceed to the Scope Tags page.

Because Defender for Endpoint only works on devices, you need to either give to a group of devices or all of them. This is possibly one time when **All Devices** is useful.

- Finally, click on **Create**.
- From the menu, we can now click on the **Microsoft Defender for Endpoint** link to make sure everything is connected.

You can also find more settings here for Android and iOS devices that aren't handled by Intune. Check them out to see if they meet your needs and turn them on as needed.

Set up Application Control

Application Control is a new tool of Intune that adds to the functionality of Windows Defender Application Control (WDAC) while making deployment easier. There are two ways to deploy Application Control: through a GUI with boxes to check or through an XML file made for WDAC. If you want more precise control, you can use the Microsoft WDAC wizard to help you make the file instead of the GUI we will be using in this case. We must first enable Managed Installer before we can create our policy. This lets the Intune Management extension load apps without any problems.

To set it up in your environment, do these things:

- Go to **Endpoint Security** and click on **App Control for Business**.
- Click the **Managed Installer** tab at the top and then click Add.

- Click **Add** in the fly-out menu.
- Press "**Yes**" to make sure you want to add managed installer.
- We can create our policy now that this has been enabled. Create a Policy by selecting **App Control for Business**.
- From now on, things will look normal because this uses the normal **Unified Settings catalog.**
- Type in the **name and description** of your policy, then click **Next**.
- The **GUI** will be used on the next screen. So, choose **Use built-in controls** for the format of the configuration settings.
- This will change the way some choices are shown (again, this will look like the Settings catalog):
    - **Turn on app control policy to trust Store apps and Windows components:** Here, you can only choose between **Enforce** and **Audit**. If you set it to **Audit**, it will keep track of events but not stop any programs from running.
    - Select additional guidelines for app trust:
        - **Trust apps with good reputation**: This lets Microsoft Intelligent Security Graph trust apps.
        - **Trust apps from managed installers**: This lets AppLocker let certain installers work, like Configuration Manager.
- The two extra rules should be left empty for this case because we will only use Intune for this. When the settings for your environment are ready, click Next.
- Click **Next** because we don't need scope tags here.

For the most part, we want to set all security policies at the device level. However, this is an exception. All apps, even single ones that IT needs for debugging or one-time installs, will have to be installed through Intune if we give this to all devices. So that doesn't happen, we're going to give at the user level so that we can make exceptions for IT support staff as needed. Fill in the blanks in the groups as needed, then click "Next."

- Finally, check to make sure everything is right, and then click **Create**.

CHAPTER 5

MANAGING IOS DEVICES WITH INTUNE

This chapter examines iOS device management, setting device policies to handle company-owned and controlled devices, and app security policies to safeguard your user-owned **bring-your-own-device (BYOD)**. We will use **Apple Business Manager (ABM) (or Apple Education)** for our business devices. We will also go over how to set up Intune to work with ABM and how to deploy apps using the Volume Purchase Program (VPP). Lastly, we will sign up both a **managed** device and a **bring-your-own-device** (**BYOD**) device.

Important notes

Apple devices need you to keep an eye on when the certificates need to be renewed and write them down somewhere to remember you. You could also use Azure Automation to make the alerts happen on their own. Your devices can connect to the Intune MDM service through the MDM push certificate. You can call Apple directly within 30 days of the expiration date to renew it if this one does. If they can't or after 30 days, the only thing left to do is wipe and re-enroll all of your devices. Yes, this is a full wipe, which means all the info is gone. To join your devices for the first time, you need a registration code. Create a new enrollment page and move your devices to it if this one runs out. Even though it's not as bad as a wipe, it can make the devices look less healthy in the Intune portal. Application deployment to devices is done with the Apple VPP certificate. It will be impossible for users to download and install any new apps after that one ends. It's not a big deal, and they're easy to change, but you might waste time trying to figure out why an app won't run and not see this as the problem. The settings you choose for your device restrictions/settings catalog policy should be specific to your needs so that you can get the best protection without hurting the user experience. The App Store, iCloud, and other services should be blocked to begin with.

Configuring a connector between Apple and Intune

A connection to connect Intune to ABM or Apple Education needs to be set up before devices can be added or changed. Sign in to your ABM account and go to your account settings before you start. We can add an MDM server from this point on. We will be moving between the two when setting the certificates, so it is worth having Intune in a separate tab.

Here are the steps to follow:

- Go to Devices and then iOS in the Intune portal.
- Next, click on **iOS/iPadOS Enrollment**.
- You will see that this screen only has one choice, which is Apple MDM Push certificate. Click on that.

- Check the box in the pop-up window and then download the CSR certificate.
- After that, click on the link that says "Create your MDM push Certificate." This will take you to the Apple portal.
- Press "**Create a certificate.**"
- Click Accept after checking the box.
- Put the CSR that we got from the Intune portal online.
- Write down the expiration date or put a note somewhere to remember you, and then click Download.

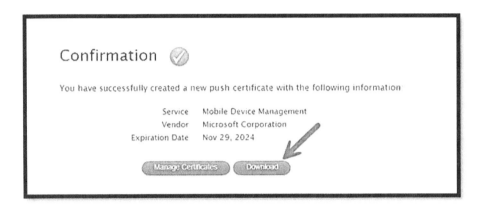

Put in your Managed Apple ID (don't use your own Apple ID), select the certificate to upload, and click "Upload." In the same panel, you should now see a success message.

Now Intune is linked to ABM, and as you can see in the image above, the state should change to "Active." This is the first step in deploying devices.

Configuring an Apple VPP token

Now that our settings are connected, we need to set up our VPP token so that we can deploy an app.

Getting started

For Apple Business Manager, open one tab and for Intune, open the other tab. For certificates, we will switch between them again.

How to do it...
- Go to the preferences in Apple Business Manager and click on Payments and Billing.
- Get the content token at the bottom of the page.
- Now go back to Intune, click on Tenant Administration, and then click on Connectors and Tokens.
- Click on **Apple VPP Tokens**.
- Go to the top and click **Create**.
- Type in your name and Apple ID, then upload the certificate you saved earlier and click Next.
- We can leave the top choice as "No" since this is the only MDM server we have.
- Select the region, the account type (usually Business, unless you're setting for a school), and whether you want to accept automatic app updates. Finally, click Next after agreeing to the terms:

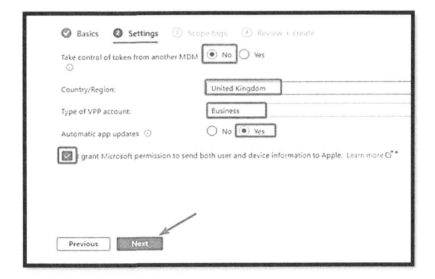

- When you get to the Scope tags tab, click Next.
- Make sure everything is right, and then click Create.

Adding enrollment profile tokens

Setting up an enrollment profile token is the last thing that needs to be done before we can enroll devices. After that, we set up ABM to use this token when deploying devices.

- Click on Devices first, then iOS/iPadOS.

- Next, click "Enroll in iOS or iPadOS."
- Press "Enrollment program tokens."
- At the top, click "Add."
- Pick "Agree" and download the public key, which we will need in Apple Business Manager.
- **Follow this link to get to Apple Business Manager:**

- In your profile in Apple Business Manager, click "Add" next to "Your MDM Servers."
- Type in a name; upload the certificate, and then click "**Save**."

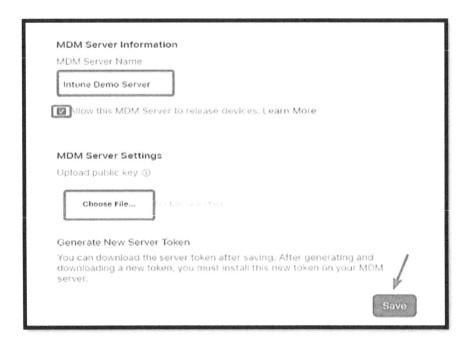

- Click **Download Token.**
- Go back to the Intune portal and enter your Apple ID. Then, choose the certificate you just downloaded and hit Next.

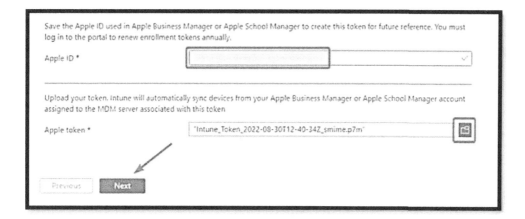

- Finally, make sure everything is right and click "Create."
- Now there are two steps to take for enrollment. To begin, go to the Apple Business Manager portal and click on MDM Server Assignment.
- Click on Edit.
- For each type of applicable hardware, select your MDM server and click Save.
- **Now go back to the Intune site and click on the program token for your new enrollment:**

- Press on Profiles.
- Click **"Create profile"** and pick **"iOS/iPadOS."**
- Fill out the form and click **"Next."**

On the next screen, you can choose between these:

- **User affinity**: This is where you can choose whether devices are linked to a specific person **(Enroll with person Affinity)**, don't have a user, like a kisok **(Enroll without User Affinity)**, or are shared devices **(Enroll with Microsoft Entra shared mode)**. **Enroll with User Affinity** is the option because we are setting a standard user device.

This will bring up some new choices for you to choose from. The first thing to think about is the way of authentication. You can either use Setup Assistant with current security or install and use Company Portal to verify users.

- **Setup Assistant with modern authentication** Setup Assistant with current security is more likely to work, so that's what we'll use in this case. Additionally, this lets you use your Entra ID details for needed login during the out-of-box experience (OOBE) before you can reach the device's home screen. It is also needed to sign up for Just in Time.

People don't need an Apple ID to run the app because we want to use the VPP.

No matter what login method was chosen, make sure that **Supervised** is set to "**Yes**." This will let you configure an uncontrolled device in more ways. Users cannot delete the name from the device while enrollment is locked. Setting **Sync with computers** to **Deny All** is what you should do unless you are using Apple Configurator:

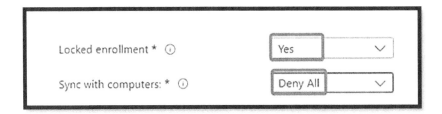

- Finally, you can set the Device Name Template. This can be any plain text or the variables {{SERIAL}} and {{DEVICETYPE}}.
- Turn on cellular data for any eSIM devices that can do so (if you choose "Yes," you will need your carrier's server URL). Press **Next**.
- On the next screen, you can choose what choices are offered during setup and enter the contact information for IT in case there are any problems.
- This will help your users get set up faster and keep their devices safe. Hide as many setup screens as you can.
- A passcode and the ability to use Touch ID and Face ID should be enough.
- After you've changed the settings, click Next.
- Take a look at the settings again, then click **Create**.
- The last step is to click **Set default profile.**
- Click OK after you select the profile you just made. After creating all of these settings, any devices that have been added to Apple Business Manager will be immediately added to Intune and set up with the enrollment profile code that was made.
- If you need to, you can directly give a profile to a device by clicking Devices in the token, picking out the device, and clicking the **Assign profile** button.

Configuring iOS policies using the settings catalog

The link between ABM and Intune is now complete. We could enroll devices right now if we wanted to, but we need to set up any policies or apps first because we haven't done that yet. Either the settings catalog or device restrictions can be used to set up policies. They both set up the same settings. It's more current to use the settings catalog, but either way will work. We will use the settings catalog in this section and device restrictions in the next one.

How to do it...

- Go to the Intune console and click on Devices. Then, click on iOS/iPadOS.
- Click on Configuration Profiles and then click on New Policy.
- Choose Settings catalog from the drop-down menu and click Create.
- As always, give it a name and a description, and then click Next.

You will now see the setting picker that we talked about earlier when we created your Windows profile. You can choose the settings that work best for your environment here. As more settings are added, this list will keep growing, so what is on it now may get longer as more are added. To use this as an example, we will set up a few device restrictions that will fit the strategy we will set up in the next section.

- Once you've changed the settings, hit Next:

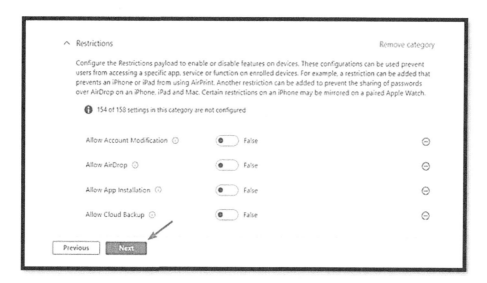

- We don't need scope tags, so click Next.

According to our choice, we can give this. You could choose all devices and create a dynamic group for device restrictions, or you could just use a basic user or device-based group. Usually, these kinds of settings will be the same across the estate. Using a dynamic group or filters will make handling the groups faster and lower the chance that a device will be given out without the restrictions being put in place.

One way to use a dynamic group is to use **enrollmentProfileName equals xxx**, where xxx is the profile name we set up earlier, or **deviceOSType equals iOS**. You can also use the name of the enrollment profile as a filter and choose to only see devices that run iOS or App Store.

- After Assignment, click Next.
- Last, make sure everything looks good, and then click Create.

Configuring iOS policies using device restrictions

The steps above showed you how to use the new settings catalog to create a new profile for your iOS devices, but you can also use a device restrictions policy. Using the device restrictions profile type, we will show you how to set up and automate your strategy here.

How to do it…
- As before, go to the Intune console and choose Devices. Then, choose iOS/iPadOS.
- Click on **Configuration Profiles** and then click on **New Policy**.
- Select Templates and then Device restrictions this time instead of Settings Catalog. Press "**Create**."
- As always, fill in the general information and click Next.

All of the device restrictions are grouped here, but you can't search for them like you can in the settings catalog. We'll change the same three settings as before to stop iCloud backups, the App Store, and AirDrop. You can find these settings in Cloud and Storage, the App Store, and Connected devices respectively. After that, click Next:

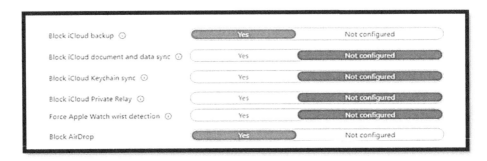

We are taken straight to the assignments page because you can't set a scope tag on a device restrictions policy. The older approach is the same way. Filtering can also be used here. Click Next after you've made the assignment.

- Finally, make sure everything is right and click "Create."

Deploying applications via Apple VPP

We have set up our limits and are now sure that the devices are safe, but our users will be upset if they can't get to the App Store and there aren't any apps available centrally. Because Apple VPP applications are the best for deploying apps in a business setting, this section will mostly talk about them.

To be informed of what is offered, it is important to cover the other application options:

- **iOS store app**: This adds apps that are just linked to the App Store. Users will need an Apple ID, and your restriction policy should be set up so that the store is not blocked. This means that users can install anything they want.
- **iOS/iPadOS web clip**: This makes the home screen of the device have a link to a web app.
- **Web link**: This adds a web link to the home screen of devices.
- **Built-in app**: These are specially chosen and approved apps that you can use without going through the App Store. They are also already set up to protect apps.
- **Line-of-business apps**: These steps will show you how to deploy custom iPad apps (up to 2 GB) to your controlled devices.

Getting started

Starting with logging in to your Apple Business Manager account and making sure that all of your information is correct. This includes setting up a payment method if you want to add any paid apps. After that, click on Apps and Books. Once you get to this screen, keep going with the section.
How to do it...

- First, look for your application. We are going to use Microsoft Authenticator to make sure that our users are set up for MFA (multi-factor authentication). After that, do these things:
- On the results pane, click on the app.
- Select your MDM server from the drop-down box, type in how many licenses you need, and click "Get." Look up at the top and see that it says "Device Assignable." Keeping this in mind is important during application assignments.
- If you have less than 5,000 licenses, the app should show up in the Intune console almost right away. Every day at 13:00 (PST), orders are processed between 5,000 and 19,999. At 16:00 (PST), more than 20,000 orders are processed.
- We will speed this up by syncing the VPP just to be safe.
- To get to Connectors and tokens in the Intune console, go to Tenant management.
- Click on **Apple VPP Tokens**.
- You might have to scroll down to find the three dots to the right of the token. Click those, and then click **Sync**:

- Click on **Apps** and then **iOS/iPadOS**.

- Your app should be on the list, but it shouldn't be assigned yet. Choose the app by clicking on it.
- Press on **Properties**.
- Click on **Edit** next to **Assignments**.

You will notice that, unlike Android, you don't have the choice **"Available for unenrolled devices."** This is because of the licenses we talked about earlier. You can choose required (which means forced installation), Available (which means self-service), or Forced Uninstall. We are going to force installation on all devices in this case because we want all users to have the app right away.

- **Once the assignment has been added, the following choices will be shown:**

The type of license is the most important one here. Our users no longer need an Apple ID because we made it so. So, we need to make sure we use **Device licensing**. If you click on any of the blue text links, a pop-up menu with more choices will appear. You can change these settings as needed. In this case, we don't want the app to be wiped unless the device is taken out of control. We also don't want it to be saved up because it saves passwords.

Click OK when you're done setting up your needs:

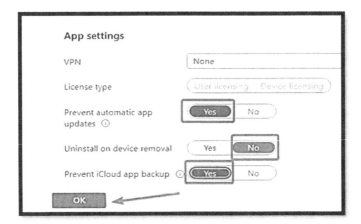

- Click Review and Save now.
- Make sure everything looks good, then click "Save."

We don't use Create because we're just making changes to an application assignment and not making something new.

Configuring iOS update settings

We might also want to handle software updates for our iOS and iPadOS devices in the same way that we handle feature updates for our Windows devices. This could entail ensuring they are always up to date, limiting devices to a certain version, or indicating when to run an update. We do this with the help of an update policy. It's important to note that this doesn't stop users from looking for and loading updates on their own, but you can allow them to wait up to 90 days by setting device limits (either in the settings catalog or a device restrictions policy).

How to do it...

- Select iOS/iPadOS from the Devices menu to create the new policy.
- Now choose Update policies for iOS and iPadOS and click Create profile.
- As usual, give it a name and a description, then click Next.

We set the policy on the next screen. You can choose which version of the OS to run on your devices from the first choice. If you leave it on Latest update, the latest version that works with your device will be installed. You can also restrict this to older versions if you need to for a specific program. You can also tell Intune to update choices when the device next checks in, or you can make a plan that only includes certain apps or all of them. You could make your busy hours match a normal work day, from 8 a.m. to 8 p.m., and then decide that you only want updates to run at odd times, like at night. In this case, set to Update outside of planned time. These could also be on-call devices, in which case you would want to set them up during the day so they are ready to go when the office is closed. Choose Update during scheduled time in this case. At our next check-in, we'll install the most recent set of changes.

- Click Next when you're done setting up your environment.
- This is not the right place to use scope tags, so click Next on the next screen.

Examine your estate and user base carefully when considering your assignments. A one-size-fits-all strategy might not work for you because you can have different change policies. You can use All Users or All Devices here if all of the devices are set up and used the same way, but it might be better to make groups. For the same reason, staff who are on call or work shifts might need a different plan than office workers who only use the device during the workday. Do not forget to use Exclusions as well. You could give All Users a catch-all role, but make sure there are exceptions for users who need slightly different settings. However, you should never mix user and device assignments. Don't forget to carefully think about your leaders and anyone else who might need the device during or after work hours. Especially when putting in new systems like Intune, it is best to check first before making any big changes or policies. Sometimes getting people to like your setup is just as hard as making it work.

- We are giving configurations to the Intune-Users group in this case.
- After that, click Next. Lastly, check the settings one last time to make sure they are right, and then click Create.

Configuring an app protection policy

Device restrictions only work on fully registered company devices, so they can't help our bring-your-own-device (BYOD) devices. Like with Android devices, we want to set up app security policies to make sure that user-owned devices store data safely. iOS doesn't have multiple profiles like Android does. This means that even though the data is safe, it is not as separated on the device.

Getting started

The Conditional access policy set up in the Android app protection policy worked on both Android and iOS devices. If you haven't already, read the Android section and set up the policy correctly instead of going through the steps in this section. You can use this to make sure that your devices will only join if the app is policy-managed.

How to do it…

1. To begin, we need to go to Apps and click on App Protection Policies.
2. Click Create Policy and choose iOS/iPadOS from the list that appears.
3. As always, name and explain your policy. The platform is already chosen based on the choice made in the drop-down box. After that, click Next.

We can pick which apps to protect here. Click the text that says +Select public apps or +Select custom apps to protect certain apps. If not, change the drop-down choices to fit your needs.

4. We will pick All Microsoft Apps and click Next in this case.
5. On the next screen, we set the settings for protecting the data that is stored in these apps. You can set these up based on what your company needs. Most of the time, these settings are good to start with:
   - **Backup org data to iTunes and iCloud backups**: Set this to Block. That way, you won't have to think about another hack.
   - **Send org data to other apps**: This should be set to policy-managed apps since we don't want data to leave the device for work. If you need to, you can add exceptions here.
   - **Save copies of org data**: Set this to Block and choose OneDrive and SharePoint to save copies of organization data. Since this is an unsecured device, we don't want data on it, but you can choose Box if it's okay in your settings.
   - **Transfer telecommunication data to**: This should be set to "None," but users might complain if they can't copy and paste a phone number, so it's worth considering.
   - **Receive data from other apps**: This should be set to either Policy Managed Apps or All Apps with Incoming org Data.
   - **Restrict cut, copy, and paste between other apps**: This should be set to policy-managed apps with paste in (restrict within the bubble).
   - **Encrypt org data**: Make sure this setting is set to "Require."

- **Sync policy managed app data with native apps or add-ins**: Set this setting to Block. Keep in mind that this stops Outlook from adding contacts to the native contacts app, so be careful when using this setting.
- **Printing org data**: If someone wants to print org data, set this to "Block." There's no point in being strict if they can just print it.
- **Restrict web content transfer with other apps**: this should ideally be set to Microsoft Edge. This is up to you, but it's easier to manage one browser across multiple devices.

6. After you've changed the settings, click Next.

On the next screen, you can set the entry conditions for the apps themselves. You can't make the device ask for a PIN, but you can make the app ask for one themselves. Set these to your needs; it's usually easiest to explain to end users if they fit the company device PIN standards. The "Work or school account credentials for access" setting is one to keep an eye on here. These will be asked for by users if you set this to require and also Require fingerprints.

7. **Set as required and click Next. You can set more conditions for viewing the program on the next page, which includes the following:**
   - Max PIN attempts: This is the most times a wrong PIN can be entered. You can erase the files or change the PIN.
   - Offline grace period: This is the amount of time you give people to get back to the data after you stop access for a certain number of minutes or days.
   - Disabled account: You can shut it down or let people in.
   - Minimum app version: The bare minimum version that can be used. You can Block access, Wipe data, or just Warn.
   - Min SDK version: Can be set to Block access, Wipe data, or Warn.

You can also put limits on the device itself, such as the ones below:

- Devices that have been jailbroken or "rooted": You can disable access or delete data.
- If you set a minimum or maximum OS version, you should either warn, block access, or delete data. If you do set this, make sure you keep an eye on it.
- Minimum patch version: warn, block access, or delete data.
- Device model(s): Don't let anything through; block or delete it. Because it's an allow list and not a block list, be careful when you add to it.
- Maximum allowed device threat level (Secured, Low, Medium, or High): Block or wipe data. This needs a Defender for Endpoint connection.
- Primary MTD service: For the main MTD service, choose either Defender for Endpoint or Mobile Threat Defense (non-Microsoft). This is your device's antivirus.

After you've changed the settings, click Next. The settings that were used in this case can be seen below:

8. On the Scope Tags page, click Next.
9. The next screen will show that we can't apply this policy to the All Users or All Devices virtual groups. We don't know anything about the devices themselves, so this policy is also based on the person. Give it to the Intune Users group. After that, click Next.
10. Last, make sure everything looks good. It will have added key links to include and exclude by itself to the policy. After that, click Create.

You may have seen that the menu has more settings under "App protection policies." We will go over those now to help you understand better.

Looking at app configuration policies

App configuration policies can be used at either the device level or the application level to set up settings that are special to an app if the app supports this. For example, setting up the Outlook app or line-of-business apps is one example. It will depend on the app whether you can use a setup creator or type in the raw text, which could be S/MIME/XML, JSON, or something else. For some apps, like Outlook, the setup creator has all the settings you need, while for others, it only has text boxes. Make sure you know what to put in them.

To give you an idea, let's look at Outlook as an example:

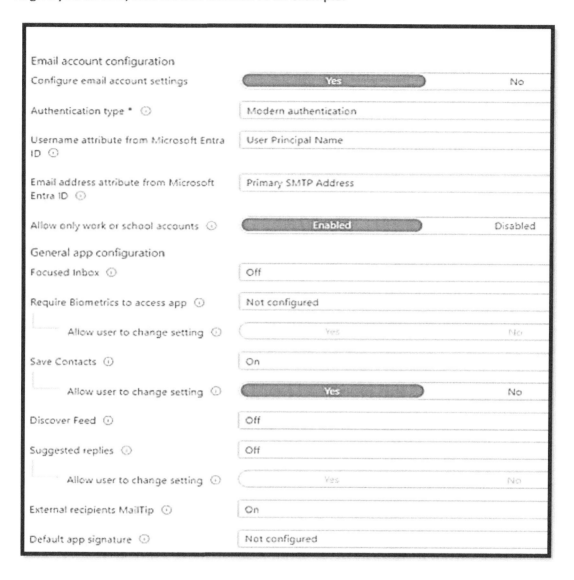

For example, you have to enter the settings for Microsoft Word manually:

Selecting the settings in Outlook will automatically fill in the following values:

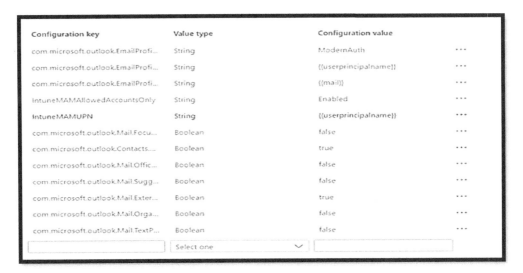

Enrolling your device – corporate

Now that our setting is set up, we can begin registering our devices, starting with those that belong to and are controlled by the company.

Getting started

First, make sure that you have either Apple Education Manager or (ABM) of a fully reset iOS or iPadOS device signed in.

Follow these instructions:

- First, make sure your device's language and region are set.
- Click set up manually on the Quick Start screen.
- If you need to, connect to your Wi-Fi network or use your phone's data plan.
- The screen for remote management will then show up. Press Next.
- Use your login information to log in, and then click Next.
- You will be asked to set and confirm a PIN if your policy needs one after you log in.
- Finally, after a few minutes, you will see your home screen with all of your deployed apps.

There's more

As of recently, Just in Time enrollment for iOS and iPadOS has been added to Intune. This uses the single sign-on (SSO) plugin and lets you sign in to any app that works with it to finish registration and a safety check.

Enrolling your device – BYOD

Allowing personal devices to be registered doesn't help because Android and iOS are different in ways like no work profile, VPP, and Google Play. Instead, using app security policies is better. Because of this, we will only show you how to join using app security in this section.

Getting started

To get to Microsoft Store apps, you will need to set up and log in to an Apple iOS or iPadOS device with an Apple ID.

How to do it...

- Open up the App Store and look for an app. We are going to use Microsoft Word in this case. Click Open when you're done installing.
- Click Existing Microsoft 365 Users? Sign In.
- Type in your email address and click "Next."
- Type in your password and click "Sign In."
- Once you have signed in, you will see the message below. To restart the app, click OK:

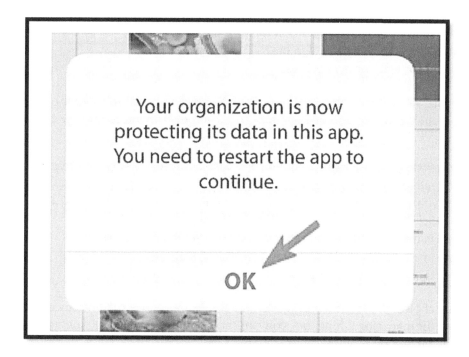

- You will be asked to set a PIN whenever you use the app to open or create a document. You will also be told about any PIN limits that are part of your app's security setting.
- Do the same things with any other apps for organization.

CHAPTER 6

MANAGING ANDROID DEVICES WITH INTUNE

Setting up a managed Google Play account

We need to connect Intune to a managed Google Play account before we can set up any Android policies or settings. Following that, we will use this to join devices and send out apps. You don't need a Google account to do this; we can make one for you during the process. It would be best if it was an Android Enterprise account. Another good idea is to use a shared or general account instead of one that is linked to a specific employee.

Follow these steps:

- First, we need to go to the Intune tab and click **Devices**.
- After that, click **Enrollment**. If you're using the old site, click **Enroll Devices.**
- Click on **Android** now.
- Click on **Managed Google Play**.
- Click the Launch Google to connect now button and check the box to say you agree to the terms.
- Click one of the Sign In buttons in the pop-up box.
- Click **Create Account**, not Sign in.
- Select "**For work** or **my business**."

You can create a new Gmail account here or set it to use one related to your name (don't use a personal account, though). You will need to prove you own the account if you choose to use a custom email.

- We will only use a Gmail account for this case because it is easy. After you've put in all the required information, click Next.
- Yes, you will need to verify with a phone number for safety reasons. Type in a number and click "Next." This doesn't need to be a cell phone.
- Type in the verification code that was sent to you and clicks "Next."
- Type in your recovery information and click "Next."
- Click Skip on the screen that says "Get more from your number."

The next few choices are for advertising preferences. Express will work fine since this account will only be used for managing Intune, but you can set it up more precisely if you need to. Select the choice you want and click "Next."

- Click "I agree" to agree to the rules.
- We don't want to make a business profile here, so click "Not Now."
- Press "Get Started."

- Type in information about your company and click Next.
- Fill out the form with your contact information (optional), and click "**Confirm**" to agree to the rules.
- Finally, click the **"Complete Registration"** button.

Now the window will close, and you'll be back in Intune, where you can make sure the link is still live:

You have now successfully linked your tenant to Google Play. We can now use this to set up our devices and deploy applications.

Configuring enrollment profiles

We can set up a profile that lets devices sign up now that our Google Play account is linked. When setting up a new device, this will give us a QR code and a text code that we can use.**First, we need to know what all the choices on the Android device enrollment screen mean before we start creating a profile:**

- **Zero-touch enrollment**: This is a way to add a lot of devices to your profile at once, without having to set up any steps during device setup and enrollment. It works like Apple iOS and Apple Business Manager Automated Device Enrollment (ADE). It needs certain devices that must be signed up for the service by the dealer or service provider. One well-known example is Samsung Knox, which you can set up and use for free. Android Zero Touch works on devices that aren't Samsung as well.
- **Personally-owned devices with work profile**: For personal devices with a work profile, this button only brings up an information page that can't be changed. When a user enrolls a personal device through the Company Portal, the apps will be added to a different profile on the device to protect the data they hold. By default, it is turned on.
- **Corporate-owned dedicated devices**: These are kiosk-style devices that don't have a unique user given to them.

- **Corporate-owned, fully managed user devices**: These are the most typical accounts for regular users who are given a fully managed business phone. In this section, we will configure this character ring.
- **Corporate-owned devices with work profile:** This is for a device that is owned by the company but can also be used for personal things. The apps on this type of device are stored in a work profile to keep the data on it safe.
- **AOSP Corporate-owned, user-associated devices:** These are fully managed user devices, but they are for Android devices that run AOSP instead of Google Play. If you have these devices, your gear provider will let you know. Most of the time, they are made for special uses, like the ones made by Zebra.
- **AOSP Corporate-owned userless devices:** This is for kiosk devices that don't run Google Play services and are owned by AOSP.
- **Android Administrator Personal and corporate-owned devices with device administrator privileges:** This way only works for old devices and company-owned ones that have device administrator rights. It shouldn't be used on new devices.

Now that we know what each part does, we will set up a profile for totally controlled, corporate-owned individual devices in this section:

- First, click on corporate-owned, fully managed user devices.
- Press "Create profile."

The process of making a profile is very easy. You only need to give it a name and a description; there are no other settings to change or assignments to make.

- Type in your Name and, if you want, a Description value, then click Next.
- Even though there isn't much to look over here, it's still a good idea to do so. After that, click the Create button.
- Now, your profile will show up in the list. The tokens are only good for 90 days after which you will need to create a new one. Of course, you can use the automation steps to have something like an Azure Runbook do this for you automatically. Click on the page that was just made.
- So, click on Token.

You will find your QR code and token here, which you can give users to enroll their devices. You can also revoke a token and export it in JSON format if you need to.

Adding a Google Play application

It's best to talk about application deployment first since we will need apps in the tenant for both device restrictions and OEM policies. Because controlled Google Play apps are the best way to get apps into a business setting, this section will mostly talk about them. **It's important to cover the other program choices so that we know what's out there:**

- **Android Store app:** This adds apps that are just linked to the Play Store. For users to be able to leave the store open, you will need to limit what they can do with their Google account. Users can then add anything they want.

- **Managed Google Play app**: This adds a well-run app that doesn't need a Google Play account. Only apps that have been approved can be allowed to use the store.
- **Web link**: Puts a web link on the home screen of devices.
- **Built-in app**: "Built-in app" refers to pre-approved and hand-picked apps that can be used without going through the Play Store. These are also the apps that have App Protection set up already.
- **Line-of-business app**: This is how custom APK links were sent to devices used by Android device administrators. When you use Enterprise, you should add it to the secret Google Play Store. The name of the app package needs to be unique, and not just in your setting. It needs to be unique across all of Google Play.
- **Android Enterprise system app**: This is used to install built-in apps, usually ones from the maker. You need to add the full name of the program, like com. Microsoft.word.

We can move on and add our first managed Google Play app now that we know about all the different types of apps.

- To begin, click on Apps.

NOTE: When you join the controlled Google Play Store, Intune immediately adds the apps that you need to enter a device. There is Microsoft Intune, Microsoft Authenticator, Microsoft Managed Home Screen, and Microsoft Intune.

- After that, click on **Android**.
- At the top, click "**Add**."
- Choose **Managed Google Play** app from the list and click on Select.
- This will bring up the Play Store in the Intune app.
- Look for the app that you want to deploy. Microsoft Outlook will be used because it is popular in most places. In the search results, click on the app.
- Press the "**Approve**" button.
- You need to make sure you agree to the rights before you click "Approve."
- Now you will be asked what should happen by default if those rights change. Select the option that works best for you (keep it allowed when the app asks for new permissions or remove approval when the app asks for new permissions) and click "Done."
- **The app will be approved. You can still turn it down or change the settings you chose before, though:**

- Finally, to add the app to Intune, we need to click the Sync button at the top.
- It will take a few minutes for the app to show up in Intune. One thing to keep in mind is that it hasn't been given yet, so we need to click Microsoft Outlook.
- Click on Properties.
- Click on Edit next to Assignments.

You can do one of these things:
- Required: This will load the app immediately on all managed and enrolled devices. It can be sent to groups of users or devices, or the virtual group All Users/All Devices.
- Available for enrolled devices: This shows the app in the Company Portal for devices that have been enrolled. Since the app is already out there, it can only be aimed at users.
- Available with or without enrollment: This shows the apps in the Company Portal even if the device isn't enrolled in Intune (like a BYOD using MAM). It can only be aimed at users, and those users must have an Intune license.
- Uninstall: This gets rid of the app without asking you first. It can be aimed at either the person or the device.

Because we want to show both corporate and BYOD, we will launch both with and without enrolling our Intune users into the Entra ID group. You can change the priority for updates and choose whether the assignment is included or not by clicking Included or Default under Update Priority. Click Review + Save when you're done setting everything up.

- Click Save when you're sure that everything on the review screen is right.

Configuring a device restrictions policy

We can now join a device, but it won't be set up in any way, and it will work the same way as any other off-the-shelf device. To give them a full business experience, we need to set up a strategy to control them. Because Android policies have not yet been moved to the Settings store, we will set up a device limits policy with some basic settings to get you started. More settings will be in the PowerShell script and the JSON that comes with it.

How to do it…

- To begin, go to the Intune page and click on **Devices**.
- After that, click on **Android**.
- Now, click on **Configuration Profiles**.
- Last, click +Create | +New policy to add a profile.
- Under **Fully Managed, Dedicated, and Corporate-Owned Work-Profile**, select **Android Enterprise** and then **Device Restrictions**. After that, click **Create**.
- Give your policy a name and a description, and then click **Create**.

The next screen shows a list of all the settings that Android devices can have. Note the headers because some settings only work with certain types of devices (for example, kiosk settings only work with dedicated devices).

- **For our fully managed, user-assigned devices, these are some suggested settings:**

- Wi-Fi access point configuration: Block.
- Tethering and access to hotspots: Block.
- USB file transfer: Block.
- External media: Block.
- Factory reset protection emails: This allows you to restrict factory reset to approved admins only.
- Factory reset: Block.
- Notification windows: Disable.
- Locate device: Allow.
- Threat scan on apps: Require.
- Enrollment profile type – fully managed: This loads additional settings to configure the device using Microsoft Launcher. Ensure Microsoft Launcher is a required application.
- Password: Set this to whatever suits your environment. It is always recommended to disable everything from the lock screen.
- Add new users: Block.
- User removal: Block.
- Personal Google accounts: Block.
- Lock screen message: Set this to something for lost devices as an extra protection layer.
- Once your settings are set, click the "Next" button.
- Choose whether to give it to your Intune users group or All Users/All Devices and then hit Next.
- Make sure everything looks good, then click "**Create**."

Configuring an OEM policy

Most of the big Android makers also let you set up settings that are unique to your device by using a Google Play app and an OEM policy that goes with it. After that, you can use device filters to make sure that these policies and apps only run on the right devices. We are going to use the Surface Duo OEM setup for this case, so deploy the Microsoft Surface OEM tool in your settings and give it to someone.

After the application has been accepted and assigned, go to the next steps to set up the policy.

- Start by going to **Devices**.
- After that, click on **Android**.
- After that, click on **Configuration Profiles**.
- To begin, click **+Create | +New policy**.
- In the end, pick **Android Enterprise** and **OEMConfig**, then click **Create**.
- As always, give it a name and a description. To choose the OEM Config app you already deployed, hit the blue text that says "Select an OEM Config app."
- Pick out the app and click "**Select**."
- After setting up, click **Next**.

- You can choose whether to set up the settings in a graphical user interface (GUI) or by changing the JSON on the next screen.

We will keep going with the setup creator because all of Microsoft's settings are easy to use. However, you should always check which choice works best for your maker. For extra safety, we will stop Bluetooth and NFC in this case. Once the settings for your surroundings have been set, click Next:

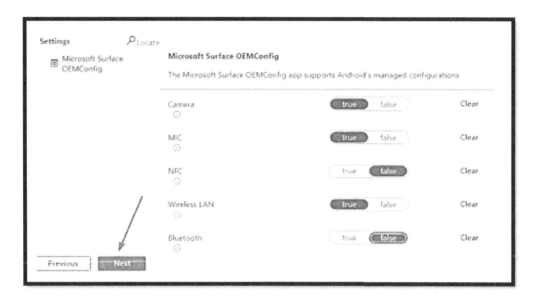

To skip the Scope tags page, click next. For assignments, pick the one that goes best with it. Pick All Devices first, then filter to just your Surface devices. This is how a Surface filter looks:

We will just click Next and give to All Devices for now. Make sure everything looks good, and then click "**Create**."

Configuring a Wi-Fi policy

In a business or office setting, you want a secure wifi network that users shouldn't connect to and can't connect to themselves. This can be done with a certificate-based link or just a secure code that staff doesn't know. A Wi-Fi strategy must be deployed to our mobile devices to accomplish this. However, keep in mind that the devices will not be aware of this new strategy until after enrollment unless you are using a zero-touch enrollment method like Samsung Knox. So, you will need to connect to the internet the first time you join and set up new devices. This could be a guest network, a 4G or 5G link, or a simple enrollment network with stringent security policies. Because an Enterprise setup needs to issue certificates, this example will only show how to set up a simple WPA2 network.

Getting ready

For this to work, you will need a safe Wi-Fi network and the WPA key. You will need to set up the certificate policies ahead of time if you want to use an Enterprise Wi-Fi network.

- Go to **Configuration profiles** under **Devices** and then **Android** to create our policy.
- After that, click **+Create | +New policy**.
- Select **Android Enterprise** as the **Wi-Fi profile type**, then click "**Create**."
- Give it a name and a description, and then click "**Next**."
- Select the **Wi-Fi type** from the list. For WEP/WPA key-based authentication, you can pick Basic. For EAP/PEAP certificate-based authentication, you can pick Enterprise. We are setting up a Basic network for this case.
- After putting in the correct information, click "Next."
- Now, give the policy to the right place. All Devices or All Users will work if the estate only has one network. If you have different networks, you might want to use group-based assignments so that IT has a less restricted network. After setting up, click Next.
- Take a look at the settings and then click **Create**.

Adding an app protection policy

What about devices owned by users who want to access their email and other company apps on their devices? We have now set policies for our corporate-owned devices to keep them safe and controlled. If we block this entirely, we will have to buy and handle a lot more business devices, which is not a good idea for most people. You could also do nothing and let them add the apps without any oversight. However, this is not a good idea for data security because you will not be able to control your company's data. We can use app security policies and enroll devices for Mobile Application Management (MAM) instead of Mobile Device Management (MDM) to do this. Both can be used for added security, but this is rare because it will add extra steps for the users on their devices, and we can assume that a controlled device is safe at the device layer. We don't want users to fully join their own devices in the Intune tenant, so it makes sense to block those devices. To make sure that uncontrolled apps can't get to any data, we will also want to connect this to an Entra conditional access policy. If you send a remote wipe to these devices, it will only wipe the managed apps and not the rest of the device. The policies for app protection can be used on all relevant apps, whether they are Microsoft apps, core apps, or specific apps.

How to do it...

First, we will talk about the application protection policy. Next, we will talk about limited access. **To show this, we will protect all Microsoft programs. What if a different option works better for you? It's as easy as dropping the menu and making your choice again:**

- To begin, we need to click on **Apps**.
- Next, we need to click on **App Protection Policies**.
- After that, click **Create Policy.**
- From the list, select **Android**.
- Type in your name and a description, then click "**Next**." The platform has already been set up for you, which you will notice.
- We can pick which apps to protect on the next screen. You need to click **+Select Public Apps or +Select Custom Apps** to protect certain apps. If it doesn't, change the choices to fit your needs.
- We will pick **All Microsoft Apps** and click **Next** in this case.
- On the next screen, we need to set the settings for protecting the data that is stored in these apps. You can set these up based on what your company needs.

Most of the time, these settings are good to start with:
- Back up org data to Android backup services: Block (one less breach to worry about)
- Send org data to other apps: Policy managed apps (we don't want info on the device to leave our company area)
- Save copies of org data: We don't want data on an unsecured device, so we'll block it with OneDrive and SharePoint chosen. Choose Box if it's okay in your setting.
- **Transfer telecommunication data to**: Any policy-managed dialer app (again, keep things under control)
- Open data into org documents: Block with OneDrive for Business and SharePoint selected. This is for putting into documents, but it can be loosened if needed.
- Restrict cut, copy, and paste between other apps: Policy-managed apps that let you write in (limit inside the bubble)
- Screen capture and Google Assistant: Block
- Encrypt org data: Require
- Encrypt org data on enrolled devices: Require
- Sync policy-managed app data with native apps or add-ins: Block (be careful with this setting because it stops Outlook from adding contacts to the local contacts)
- Printing org data: Block (this doesn't make sense if they can just print it)
- Restrict web content transfer with other apps: Microsoft Edge (this is a matter of taste, but it's easier to manage one browser across all devices)

After you've changed the settings, click **Next**. On the next screen, "**Access requirements,**" you can set the entry needs for the apps themselves. Even though you can't make the device ask for a **PIN**, you can make the app ask for one. Make these the preferred ones. To make things easier for end users to understand, it's best to match the PIN standards for company devices. On the next page, called "**Conditional launch,**" you can add more rules about how to open the app, **such as the ones below:**

- **Max PIN attempts**: How many times can a wrong PIN be entered? After that, you can either change the PIN or delete all the info.
- **Offline grace period**: How long do you let people use the data before you block access? After how many days do you delete the data?
- **Disabled account**: Block or give entry.
- **Minimum app version**: the oldest version of the app that can be used

You can also make sure the device doesn't do certain things:

- **Jailbroken/rooted devices**: Disable access or delete info.
- **Minimum or Maximum OS version:** Warn, block, or wipe data. You should keep an eye on this one if you are setting it.
- **Minimum patch version:** Warn, block, or wipe data.
- **Device manufacturer(s):** Block or delete anything that wasn't asked for. This is an "allow" list, not a "block" list, so be careful when you add to it.
- **SafetyNet device attestation:** A security API will check to see if the app and operating system are real and either warn, block, or delete data.
- **Require threat scan on apps:** warn or block them.
- **Required SafetyNet evaluation type:** hardware-backed.
- **Require device lock (low, medium, or high complexity):** Warn, block, or wipe data.
- **Minimum Company Portal version or Maximum Company Portal age:** It's important to keep an eye on the Minimum Company Portal version and Maximum Company Portal age so that you can warn, stop, or delete data. If your minimum is out of date, it will soon be useless anyway.
- **Maximum allowed device threat level (secured, low, medium, or high):** To delete or block data, you need to connect to Defender for Endpoint.
- **Primary MTD Service**: Defender for Endpoint or Mobile Threat Defense (non-Microsoft) should be your device's main MTD service. This is its antivirus.

After you've changed the settings, click Next. The settings that were used in this case can be seen in the next image:

- You will see on the next screen that we can't add this to the virtual groups "All Users" or "All Devices." We don't know anything about the devices themselves, so this strategy is also based on the user. We will give it to the Intune Users group. After that, click Next.
- The last step is to check your settings again and click Create.

Creating the conditional access policy

So far, we have our app protection policy with all of its lovely Block Access settings. However, Intune cannot stop users from accessing Microsoft 365 apps on its own. So that can happen, we need to use conditional access. In this case, we will personally create the policy so that you can understand the settings. There are new policy examples for most needs. There is an important thing to remember when setting up conditional access policies: make sure you have a break-glass account set up that is not affected by any policies. You can use this to get into the environment and fix the problem if you set a policy by mistake that keeps everyone out. A break-glass account should be a non-user account with a very strong password kept on paper in a safe place, preferably a fireproof safe. If you can, connect it to a FIDO2 key that is kept in a different safe as well. Keep in mind that this account has full access to your environment and none of your conditional access controls are in place, so it needs to be properly sealed off. **Here are the steps you need to take to get to conditional access policies:**

- You can either use the Entra portal or click Conditional Access in Endpoint Security.
- Press "**Policies**" and then "**+New policy.**"
- Give your policy a name and then click **0 users and groups selected**.

- Select **All Users** under **Include**, and then **Exclude** your break-glass account.
- In the next step, click on **No cloud apps**, actions, or authentication contexts selected.
- Select **All Cloud apps.** We want this setting to cover everything.
- Click **0 conditions selected**.
- After that, click on **Device Platforms Not Configured.**
- Set Configure to Yes. Because app security only works on Android, Windows, and iOS, we need to make this strategy only apply to those three systems.
- Click "**Done**" after selecting **Android** and **iOS**:

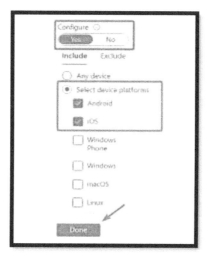

- Click 0 controls selected underneath Grant.
- Tick Require app protection policy and click Select:

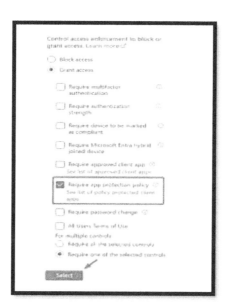

- You can set how often you want to sign in and other session-based settings with session controls. These are not needed here.
- The policy can be set to Off, Report -Only, or On at the bottom of the page. For most policies, setting it to Report-Only is the best way to see what happens. But since this is a security policy, we can just set it to On since we don't want users to be able to access apps that aren't secure. After that, click Create.

Enrolling an Android device – managed device

Now that all of our policies are set up, we can begin enrolling our devices, starting with fully managed, corporate accounts. We will require an Android device that can be wiped clean to do this. Make sure you have your previously made QR code ready and wipe your Android device to the screen where you are asked to enter your Gmail account.

How to do it…

On the screen where you need to enter your credentials, there are two choices based on how old the device is. You will need to enter **afw#setup** on older devices. **On newer devices, keep tapping the same screen:**

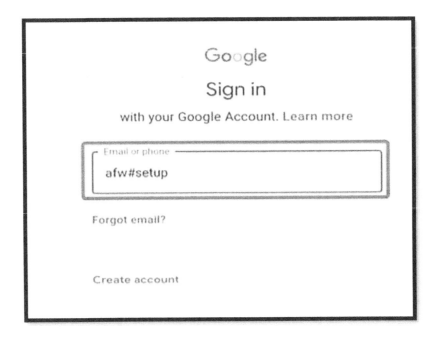

- On the screen that says "**Let's set up your work device,**" click **Accept and Continue**.
- Scan your QR code or type it in manually, then click **Accept & Continue.**
- On the privacy screen, click **Next**.
- On the Chrome screen, click "**Accept and Continue.**"

- Type in your email address and password to log in.
- Set up your screen lock.
- Adjust the settings for notifications, and then click "**Next**." We already set it up through policy, so the settings don't matter here.
- On the screen that says "Install work apps," click "**Install**."
- Once you're sure of the needed apps (which will be different for each setting), click "**Done**."
- On the screen that says "Register your device," click "**Set up**."
- On the Intune screen, click **Sign In.**
- Press the "**Done**" button.

The home screen of your device will appear. You're done! Your Android device is now enrolled.

Enrolling an Android device – BYOD

The section before this one was for corporate-owned devices. But you can't restart and enroll a device that you own without a lot of complaints. Since these are work devices, we will use the Company Portal app to install our deployed apps in the secure work profile. As you will remember, personally owned devices with a work identity are automatically activated. Based on how your system is set up, you can either let personal devices sign up with a work profile or stop them from doing so. Each has a slightly different way to sign up, so we will go over both of them here.

Getting ready…

You will need an up-to-date Android device that can connect to the Play Store and have an account that is signed in to see this.

How to do it…

First, let us see what happens if you accept personal enrollment in your tenant.

Enrolling with personal enrollment allowed

Do these things:

- Find the **Intune Company Portal** app in the Google Play Store and click "**Install**."
- When you're done, click "**Open**."
- After it loads, click Sign In.
- After adding your login information, you will be asked to set up and register your work page. Press "**Begin**."
- Check the settings for permissions and click **Continue**.
- Then there's another set of terms for you to accept and continue.
- Now the phone will set up the work profile. This process can take a few minutes. It will then show you the next screen, which you should click Next on.

- This will set up things and take you back to Company Portal. Once you have logged in again, you will be taken back to the first screen, but this time you will be able to start the work page. Press "**Continue**."
- You will be taken back to the screen where everything should be set up after about a minute. Press "**Done**."
- The operation of a work profile will now be briefly explained to you. Press **"Got It."**
- Click Open in the notification at the bottom to see the available apps. The Play Store icon with a bag next to it can also be clicked:

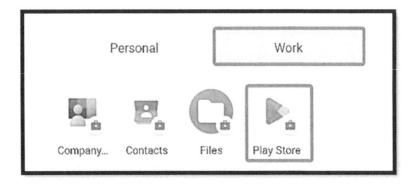

We made Outlook an open app, as you can see, and it now shows up here. It will be put in the work profile if we install it, and we can control the info that is in that profile. The icon for all work profile apps looks like a bag. Now let's look at what happens if you have personal enrollment blocked.

Enrolling with personal enrollment blocked

Company Portal is still used for this process to make sure that our app protection policies are **followed.**

The program doesn't do anything else—you can't add apps from inside it—it only acts as a middleman:

- Find Microsoft Outlook (or Word, Excel, or something else) and install it.
- After installing it, click "Open."
- The next screen will appear after you log in. Click on **GO TO STORE:**

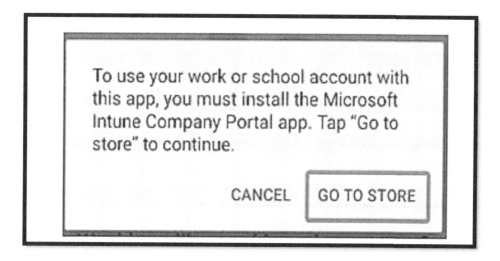

- This link will take you to the Company Portal. Click on Install. After installing it, click "Open."
- You will then be led back to Outlook, where you can continue as usual. Through the app security policy, all the info in the app is kept safe.

CHAPTER 7
MANAGING MACOS DEVICES WITH INTUNE

We will examine setting up a company device and then deploying it. It will be set up for Apple Business Manager (or Apple Education) for this. These steps will show you how to set up profiles for your macOS devices and enroll them. Using the **Volume Purchase Program**, we will also go over how to configure Intune to work with Apple Business Manager and deploy apps.

Configuring a macOS Settings catalog policy

We've looked at the different types of policies that are out there, but the settings catalog is by far the most flexible. It is constantly being updated with new settings, so this is the best way to get settings on your macOS device. One more thing that makes this policy choice better than others is that you can now export and import the settings catalog right from the UI.

Read this section to learn how to configure your devices.

To set up our first macOS policy, we will learn how to use the settings catalog:

1. In the beginning, go to **Devices** and click on **macOS**.

2. Next, go to Configuration Profiles, click **Create**, and then choose **New Policy.**
3. Click the **Create** button after selecting the **Settings** catalog.
4. Give it a name and a description if you want to, then click Next.

We have to add settings, just like on our Windows and iOS devices. You can choose the settings that work best for your environment here. Follow the same "less is more" philosophy that we used with Windows. Having many small policies is better than a few big ones that are hard to handle. To do this, we will put some simple limits on the device, secure it, and allow OneDrive Known Folder Move (KFM) and Files On-Demand. Once more, the CIS and NCSC baselines (you can find out more by clicking on the link in the "Important Notes" section) can help you with basic security. Keep in mind that many of the macOS settings we use tend to be set to "allow" instead of "block." Be careful with the words you use; you don't want to set up a strategy that lets everything through that you meant to block.

5. **As soon as the settings are right, click Next:**

- On the Scope Tags page, click Next.

Because this is a policy that restricts devices, we chose settings that will work on all of them, so we can use the "All Devices" assignment. We could even go one step further and apply a filter only to macOS devices. When making basic policies, it's best to leave out any settings that might need to be set up differently for different user groups. This is also true for any other policies. This way, you can set one standard for the whole estate and use the smaller, simpler policies to handle on/off cases that aren't part of the standard. Click Next when you're done setting up your assignment. The last step is to make sure everything looks good, and then click **Create**.

Deploying shell scripts to macOS

PowerShell scripts let you make changes to Windows devices that can't be done any other way, like using the settings catalog or a custom OMA-URI. Shell scripts can be used instead on devices that run macOS. These can be set up to run at either the system or user level. Since macOS is built on UNIX, it can set up almost anything on a device.

Getting started

We will begin with the prerequisites and things to keep in mind when using shell scripts:

Prerequisites

You must be running at least macOS 11.0 before you can do this. Your devices must be able to connect to the internet directly (no proxy servers). Scripts need to start with #!

Considerations

- Shell scripts run in parallel, so if you deploy more than one, they will all run at the same time.
- Scripts deployed as the signed-in user will run on all signed-in accounts on the device at the time the script runs.
- For user-level scripts to work, the user must be logged in.
- Any user-level scripts that run higher commands will need to be run by root.
- Although you can choose how frequently a script will run, it might run more frequently if something changes on the device (clear the cache, device restart, etc.).
- A script that runs for more than an hour will time out, stop, and be marked as failed.
- Shell scripts can't be bigger than 200 KB.

We can now create our first shell script after these are finished. This article will not show you how to make shell scripts. Instead, it will talk about how to deploy them on your devices. You will need a shell script in **.sh** file before you can start. These steps will also help you learn how to deploy a custom profile, which is what your script needs to run on devices.

How to do it...

We need to first deploy the shell script. After that, we can set up the strategy to deploy it.

Deploying a Shell script

To deploy a shell script into Intune, do these things:

1. To begin, we need to go to Devices and then macOS.
2. Go to macOS policies, click on Shell scripts, and then click on Add. Give it a name and a description, and then click Next:
3. Pick out your script by clicking the folder button.
4. The script's contents will be shown in the read-only editor below the script path on the screen. You will have to re-upload the file if you need to make changes:

```
# Define variables
usebingwallpaper=true # Set to true to have script fetch wallpaper from Bing
wallpaperurl="https://numberwang.blob.core.windows.net/numberwang/macOSWallpaper.jpg"
wallpaperdir="/Library/Desktop"
wallpaperfile="Wallpaper.jpg"
log="/var/log/fetchdesktopwallpaper.log"

# start logging

exec 1>> $log 2>&1
```

You can see the information below the script name. As you can see in the image above, we want the script to run as an administrator, so run script as signed-in user is set to No. Please don't send us any alerts. The script needs to run every day so that we can change the background.

5.   Once you have set up your script's settings, click Next:

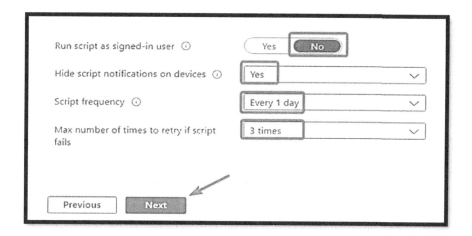

Right now we are not setting any scope tags, so click Next. Assign as needed. We'll use Intune users so that we can have different pictures for each group of users, but if it's a set corporate background, all devices with a filter will also work fine. Click Next after setting your assignments. Last, make sure everything is right, and then click "Add."

Deploying a custom profile

We just made a script that will download the wallpaper picture to the device, but we also need to tell it to use it.

To do what, we are going to deploy a custom profile:

- Start by going to Configuration Profiles. Then, click Create and then choose New policy.
- In the drop-down menu, select **Templates | Custom**. Then, click **Create**.
- Pick a name and description for your new page.

- Give the setting a name and choose whether it works for the user or the device. The only option if you choose the wrong option here is to rebuild the profile because this cannot be changed after the profile has been made.
- After you upload your file, it will show up in the window below, but it can only be read.
- The file needs to run in the device context in this case. Click Next: to continue after adjusting your settings.

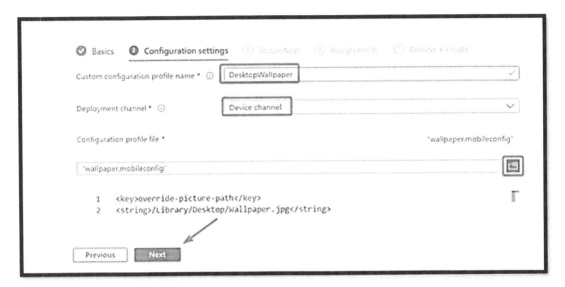

- Once more, we don't need scope tags here, so click Next.
- It is a good idea to match this assignment to the custom script that was launched earlier, and then click Next.
- Make sure everything looks good, and then click "Create."
- To go one step further, you can stop users from changing the background by going to the settings menu and setting **Allow Wallpaper Modification** to **False**.

Configuring update policies for macOS

To make the whole estate safer, we want to make sure they all have the most recent OS version, just like our Windows and iOS devices. The Software Updates template in Profiles, the Software Updates group in the Settings catalog, or a unique menu item can all be used to create an update policy for macOS. In this case, we will use the specific update policies page to keep things the same across all platforms. This way, you will always know where to find your updates. Just like with Windows devices, it's best to use deployment rings for a big macOS area so that updates can be tried before they are sent to everyone.

How to do it...

1. Go to Devices and then click on macOS.
2. Click on Update Policies for macOS after that.
3. Click on Create profile.
4. We will start by giving it a name and a description, as we always do, and then click Next.
5. On the next screen, you can choose what to do with All other updates, Critical updates, Firmware updates, and Configuration file updates.
6. **The choices you have are these:**
   - Not Configured: Do nothing.
   - Download and install: Download or install, depending on the current state.
   - Download only: Download but do not install.
   - Install immediately: Download and trigger a restart notification (this is best for userless devices).
   - Notify only: Download the updates and notify in system settings.
   - Install later: Download and defer installation (not for major OS upgrades). Selecting this option will then display the maximum user deferrals before installation and the priority (low or high) on all other updates only.

You can also set a plan that can either include or exclude devices, just like with iOS. For example, you can set a schedule that will only install when the device next checks in to Intune. The active hours could be set to 8:00 AM to 18:00 PM to catch the normal working day. You could also set it to update outside of planned time if you only want the updates to be made when it's not active. On the other hand, your users may turn off their devices at the end of the workday, so you need to force updates to happen during the workday to make sure they are installed. Choose Update during planned time in this case. At our next check-in, we'll install the most recent updates.

7. After setting up your environment, click Next.

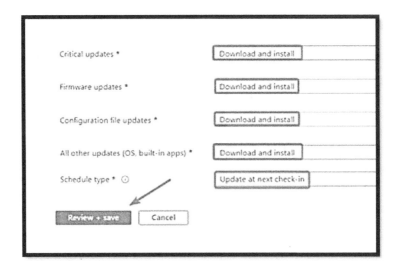

8. We don't need scope tags, so click Next once more.

Take a look at your assignments now, based on what you chose for the change policy. For various user groups or device types, you might want to create multiple policies with different settings. In our case, we will assign to Intune users, which will give us the freedom to leave out other groups as needed. You can't choose between different deployment rings like you can with Windows devices, and you also can't change the OS version like you can with Windows and iOS.

9. After setting up everything, click Next.

10. Finally, make sure everything looks good, and then click "Create."

In the Intune UI, we were able to create our update policy.

Deploying apps to macOS

Even though we have set up and protected our devices, the end users will also want some apps to be deployed. There are some choices inside Intune, such as:

- Microsoft 365 Apps: A GUI to deploy M365 apps
- Microsoft Edge: To deploy Edge version 77 and later (Chromium)
- Microsoft Defender for Endpoint: To protect your devices
- Web link: Deploy a URL to the desktop
- Line-of-business app: Deploy a custom pkg application
- macOS app (DMG): Upload and deploy a DMG-based application
- App Store app: Similar to iOS, this deploys a VPP app from the App Store

Getting started

Make sure you have a DMG file ready to deploy and that you can get to either Apple Education or ABM to deploy apps from the App Store.

How to do it...

The steps for all of these will come from Apps and then macOS apps on the Intune site.

App Store

Do what's written below:

- Go to **ABM** and click on **Apps and Books.**
- Look for the app you want and make sure it's a macOS app. We will use **GarageBand** in this case:

- Once you've clicked on the app, buy rights for your MDM and then click **Get**:

- This app should show up in Intune almost right away.
- When you go back to the Intune site, you can see the application that hasn't been given yet. To set up assignments, click on it:

Name		Type	Status	Version	Assigned
GarageBand	↑↓	macOS volume purchase pro...			No

- Go to **Properties** and click on **Edit** under **Assignments**.

Assign the application as required. Create application-specific install and uninstall groups, as is typically recommended for applications like this one. The assignments can be more general for a common app like M365 or Edge. The app can also be set as either self-service (Available) or forced install (Required). When using free apps that don't need a license, one choice is to make group members install them (only those who need to for their job) and let others install them as needed.

- Once the assignment has been added, the following choices will be shown:

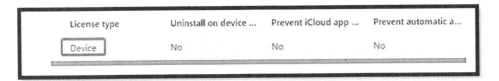

License type	Uninstall on device ...	Prevent iCloud app ...	Prevent automatic a...
Device	No	No	No

The license type is the most important choice here. Because we don't want our users to need an Apple ID to run apps, we need to make sure we pick a Device license. If you click on any of the blue text links, a pop-up menu with more choices will appear. These settings can be changed to fit your needs. In this case, we want the app to be forced, updated, and not backed up because it saves passwords and shouldn't be erased until the device is taken out of Intune control. Click **OK** when you're done setting up your needs:

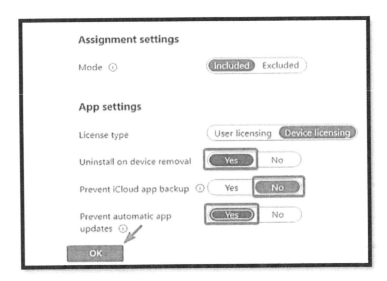

Once you're happy with your settings and assignments, click **Review** and **Save**. There is no **Create** or **Add** choice because we are making changes to an already existing app. Make sure everything looks good, and then click "**Save**."

DMG applications

When Intune first came out for macOS, you had to package apps in the .intunemac format, which is similar to how Windows Win32 apps are packaged in the intunewin format. Lucky for us, in early 2022, it became possible to directly deploy .dmg files. To follow along with this section, you will need to deploy a DMG file to your devices. For this example, we will use Adobe Acrobat Reader (if you are getting from Windows, click More Options to choose the macOS version):

Now, do these things:

- Go back to the Apps/macOS Intune page and click "**Add**."
- Choose **macOS App (DMG)** from the drop-down menu, then click **Select**.
- Choose **Select app package file**.
- In the pop-up window, choose the DMG file you downloaded earlier, then click OK.
- Fill out the rest of the application. If you let end users do this on their own, giving them a picture and topic will make it easy for them to find their way around the company site. After you've put in all the required information, click **Next**:

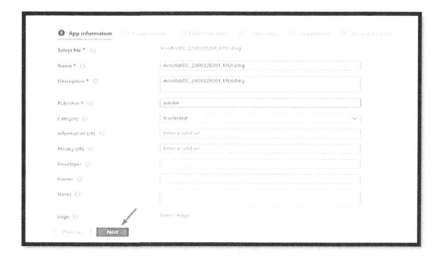

- On the next screen, you can choose which OS version the program needs to be able to run. Since the installer works on all of them, we will choose the oldest OS version.
- If you have a mixed estate, you can deploy different versions of the same app and then use device filters to make sure that only the right devices get installed when you give them.
- Click **Next** after you've chosen a version.

- We need to now look at detecting applications. First, look at or don't look at the app version. If the app updates itself, you should leave the **Ignore app version** as **Yes** so that the app can still be found after an update.
- If you choose "No," this means that the app bundle ID and version must match before the app is removed (when a person or device is added to the uninstall group). If this is set to "Yes," Intune will only look at the bundle ID and not the version.
- To get the bundle ID, put the app on a test computer and run this command in Terminal (using the exact name of the app instead of Adobe Acrobat Reader):

osascript -e 'id of app "Adobe Acrobat Reader"'

- Pay close attention to the name because the app list checks the case.
- We must enter an app version, but since we have the Ignore app version set to Yes, it will not be used. After setting up, click **Next**.

- By selecting **Next**, we can skip the Scope Tags page.
- We will use groups for required and Uninstall assignments, just like we did with the store app. Applications that are deployed by DMG don't have a self-service choice. Click **Next** when you're done adding your groups.
- Finally, make sure everything looks good and click "**Create**."

Microsoft 365 apps

Now that we've talked about the more complicated programs, we can move on to the easier, GUI-based versions of your most important Microsoft programs. Because of how applications and policies are handled, it is usually best to install Microsoft 365 apps as a Win32 app that comes with the Office Deployment Tool (ODT). **The GUI works well and doesn't have the same problems on macOS, though:**
- Create a new app in macOS apps, choose macOS from the list of Microsoft 365 apps, and then click **Select**.
- The usual application information is on the next screen, and luckily, it's all already filled in for you.
- You can choose from more choices here for Windows deployment, but this is a simple setup for macOS.

- Make any changes you want to your settings, and then click **Next**.
- Right now we don't need scope tags, so click **Next** again.
- Assign the application as required. In most cases, everyone needs these apps, but you can also use this dynamic rule to create a dynamic group that only contains users who have an Office desktop apps license.

(user.assignedPlans -any (assignedPlan.servicePlanId -eq "43de0ff5-c92c-492b-9116-175376d08c38" -and assignedPlan.capabilityStatus -eq "Enabled"))

- In this case, the deployment choices are either needed or open. You can't remove it, but unlike a DMG program, you can use self-service with available assignments.
- We're going to use the Intune-Users group and then click Next.
- Finally, make sure everything is right, and then click "Create."

Microsoft Edge

You might also want to put Microsoft Edge on your macOS devices to make control easier, keep your work going across platforms, and make it work with Defender for Endpoint. Thankfully, this is yet another simple GUI setup. Create a fresh application. Choose macOS under Microsoft Edge, version 77, and later this time from the menu. Version 77 was the change to the new Edge Chromium version. After that, click **Select**. Keep in mind that, like with M365 apps, the information is already filled in, but you can't add or change the picture this time. This is because the picture is chosen based on the next screen's channel choice. If you need to, make any changes you want and then click Next. On the next screen, you can choose between Dev, Beta, and Stable as the version of Edge to use. You should make stable the option for most of your users, but you should also give the Dev and Beta versions to test users, just like we do with OS updates. This lets you make sure that all web-based apps work properly before the updates are applied. It also lets you know ahead of time about any changes to the user interface that you might want to let your users know about.

We are going to deploy the Stable version in this case:

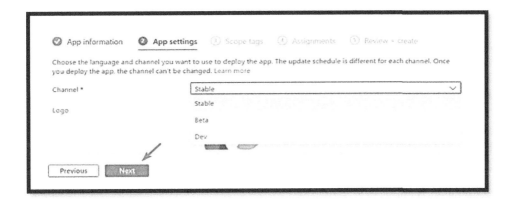

- On the Scope tags screen, press Next as usual.

- As we already talked about, you will want to have this app on all of your devices and users, but for testing reasons, you may want to use deployment rings instead. Because of this, giving the application to a group gives you more power.
- Again, keep in mind that there is no "uninstall group" choice, but you can add it to a normal "Required" installation so that users can do it themselves.
- We are going to use the Intune-Users group in this case.
- The last step is to make sure everything looks good. Then, click **Create**. Keep in mind that the badge has been added to fit the channel you picked already.

Microsoft Defender for Endpoint

The final application we may wish to deploy is Microsoft Defender for Endpoint. We can use this to keep malware away and, if we have a license, use some of the extra features, like web filtering. **NOTE:** Before you can deploy the program, you need to deploy some prerequisites to your system.

To set up Microsoft Defender for Endpoint for macOS, do the following:

- The interface is simple, just like the other Microsoft programs. Make a new app, and this time, under Microsoft Defender for Endpoint, choose macOS. After that, click Select.
- Once more, all the information is already there, even the picture, which you can't change. After making any changes that need to be made, click "Next."
- For Defender for Endpoint, there are no settings or other ways to configure it, so we go straight to the Scope tags page. Press Next.
- Once more, we can choose to deploy as needed or when possible, but we can't choose to uninstall it. As this is a security application, we want to be sure it is installed everywhere, so we are going to select All Devices.

As we already talked about, you could add a filter to include only macOS devices to make things neater. After you've put in your assignment, click Next.

- Finally, make sure everything looks good, and then click "**Create**."

Configuring a macOS enrollment profile

One more thing needs to be done before we can enroll our first macOS device: we need to set up an enrollment profile, just like we did for iOS.

Getting started

To do this, you will need to connect your Intune instance to ABM and set up an enrollment token. Please finish the following parts before moving on if you haven't already:

- Configuring a connector between Apple and Intune
- Adding enrollment profile tokens

Do what's written below:

- First, click on Devices. Next, click on macOS.
- Click macOS enrollment.
- Click on Enrollment Program Tokens.
- Press the token you created earlier:

Token name	↑	Status	Program type	↑
Intune		✓ Active	Apple Business Manager	

- Next, click on Profiles. If you already set up an iOS profile, it should be here.
- Select macOS from the drop-down menu next to Create profile.
- Type in a name and a description, and then click Next.
- We must set a few settings, just like we did with our iOS profiles.

User affinity: This tells you if the device will be linked to a person. To enroll devices that aren't kiosks, you need to choose **"Enroll with User Affinity."**

Once this is chosen, you will see an extra choice for **Authentication Method**. This is where we want to choose **Setup Assistant with modern authentication**.

Locked enrollment, says whether the user can delete the page. For business devices, this should be set to "Yes" so users can't unenroll their devices from the network.

- Click Next when you're done.
- You can choose what to show and hide on the next screen of the setup process. You don't have to use any of them, so you can just turn them all into Hidden. You do need to put the information about the area at the top. After you've set up your settings, click Next.
- We must study and create the profile right now. Make sure everything is okay, then click Create.
- Now we need to make it our default profile. All new macOS devices that come from ABM will use it by default.
- Choose Default Profile when you get back to the profiles screen.
- Under the macOS Enrollment profile, select the recently made profile, and then click OK.

Utilizing the UI, we have made our initial macOS profile in Intune.

Enrolling your corporate device

Now that our system is set up to handle and control macOS devices, we can add our first device. Since most of these are generally corporate-owned machines, this section will only talk about full ABM enrollment. For macOS devices, it is recommended that personal enrollment be turned off.

Getting started

For this section, you will need a device that has been returned to its original settings and is already signed up for either Apple Education or ABM. It should also be online.

How to do it...

When you first turn on your device, you will see a screen where you can choose your language. Click Continue after selecting the right option.

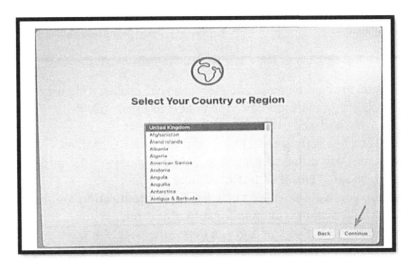

macOS will now set the language settings based on the country you chose, but you can click **Customize Settings** to make changes if you need to. After that, click **Continue**.

You might see other screens here, like **Accessibility** settings, depending on how your enrollment profile is set up.

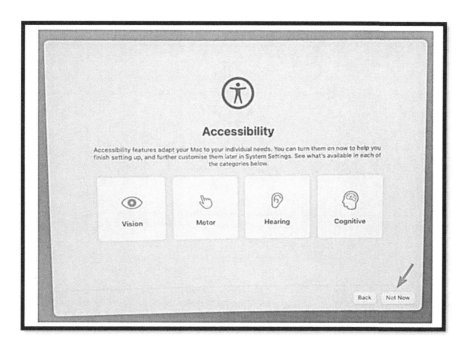

If the device doesn't already have a physical connection, you will be asked to connect to a Wi-Fi network after making any other settings. Click **Continue** after selecting your network and entering your password.

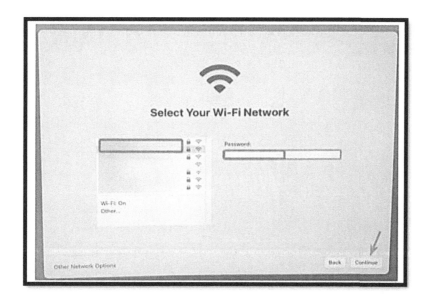

You will be asked to allow remote management, which is different from setting up an unmanaged device. Press "**Continue**."

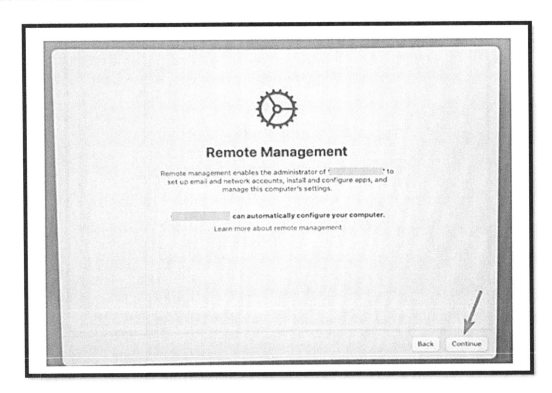

Type in your Microsoft account information (username and password). Create a user account on the device if asked, and then click **Continue**. After that, enter the account information. Last, choose your time zone, and then click **Continue**: Excellent work! You have enrolled Intune for your first macOS device.

CHAPTER 8
ESTABLISHING YOUR COMPLIANCE PROTOCOLS

Compliance Policies are ways to make sure that enrolled devices (Windows, macOS, iOS, and Android) are always controlled, up to date, and in compliance with our standards. To be considered functional in the world, devices must meet a set of rules that we can set up with these. After that, we can add a conditional access policy to make sure that devices that don't meet the requirements can't get to company data. In addition to making you safer, this lets you quickly check your estate for any big problems. We will look at what each setting needs on the device in addition to showing you how to deploy these policies. There is also the more advanced custom compliance strategy for Windows that we will talk about. Lastly, we will look at how to use conditional access to limit entry from non-compliant machines. Before we set up our policies, we need to set up one setting for the tenant. This setting tells Intune what to do with devices that don't have any compliance policies given to them. To do this, go to Devices and then Compliance. Click on Compliance policy settings after that.

These are the two settings we have:

- **Mark devices with no compliance policy assigned as:** If you don't give a policy to a device, it could be a security risk because it might not follow many settings. Setting this to "non-compliant" is always the best thing to do.
- **Compliance status validity period (days):** Here you can choose how long you will accept an old status report. For example, how many days should go by before a device is marked as not compliant if it hasn't checked into Intune? At the most basic level, think about Windows updates. If you haven't seen a computer for 30 days or more, you can assume that it is missing at least one set of updates, which could include malware updates and descriptions.

The second setting will stay at 30 days for us, and devices that don't have a policy will be marked as "Not Compliant." After setting these, click Save. Also, there is one setting that all compliance policies use, and that is what to do with non-compliant devices.

Actions for noncompliance

We must also instruct Intune on what to do when it finds devices that do not meet the requirements after selecting the compliance settings:

- **Mark device non-compliant**: You can choose how many days a device has to be before it is marked as non-compliant. As we already said, setting it to "**immediately**" might not work with all verification rules, but setting it too long raises the security risk.

- **Send email to end user**: You can also choose how many days will pass before the user gets an email telling them the device is not compliant. You can change the message that is sent and send a copy to someone else, like your IT staff. Here, you could set up more than one form that gives the person different warnings before you just block their access.
- **Add device to retire list**: Once the number of days has been chosen, the device will be put on a list to retire. Nothing will happen until the administrator retires the devices via the **Retire non-compliant** devices menu within **Compliance Policies**:

- **Send push notification to end user (Android and iOS only):** This works like email, but the message shows up on the screen and can't be changed.
- **Remotely lock the non-compliant device (iOS and Android only):** This choice keeps the person from using the device:

How to Customize Notification Templates

All systems that are enabled can send an email to the end user (and copy it to any other distribution lists) to let them know that their device doesn't meet the requirements. This can be used to let people know before the device is non-compliant.

This first section will explain how to create your template because these are cross-platform.

- To begin, go to **Devices** and then **Compliance**.
- Create a new notification by clicking on **Notifications** now.
- You must first give the template a name and choose how corporate you want it to look. The corporate information is taken from the tenant information. When you're done, click Next.
- You can change your message and language on the next screen. You can have more than one notice if you are a multinational company. Before you can click **Next** to move on, you have to set one as the default.
- Click **Next** to move past Scope tags.
- Finally, check to make sure everything is right, and then click **Create**.

Implementing a Windows Compliance Policy

Setting up compliance policies for Windows devices can be done in two different ways. We will talk about both of them here, but we will start with the easier one, which is GUI-driven.

Getting started

As we already said, we should check out the settings and what they do before we start making our policy.

Compliance Settings

We will begin by discussing the compliance settings that are currently available.

Custom compliance

Any changes made to the device can be tracked by a custom PowerShell tool and added to a compliance policy.

Device Health

The Device Health Attestation service is used by the Device Health rules. It's important to know that they need to restart the computer to report back because, among other things, they are checking the BIOS. So, if you change these settings, don't mark devices as non-compliant right away.

If you do, your new devices will lose access. Let's go over the settings that can be found under Device Health:

- Bitlocker: This program checks to see if drives are encrypted with BitLocker.
- Secure Boot: This check makes sure that Secure Boot is turned on in UEFI.
- Code integrity: looks for signs of corruption or malicious activity in drivers and firmware

Device Properties

We can choose from the following options under the name "Device Properties":

- Minimum OS version: The version of the operating system, written in the style major.minor.build.revision. Let's say we wanted the Windows 11 22H2 May 2023 version. The number would be 10.0.22621.1702.
- Maximum OS version: This is the same as the Minimum OS version, but you can also set a maximum version if you want to limit it to builds that aren't in test.
- Minimum and Maximum OS version for mobile devices: This is for Windows Mobile, so don't worry about it.
- Valid operating system builds: This lets you set more than one minimum and maximum build. One example would be adding one item for each Windows 10 and 11 versions, with the minimum set to the most recent approved version. This would only work with versions that are still supported.

Configuration Manager Compliance

- If **Configuration Manager** and your environment work together, set **Require device compliance from**
- For **Configuration Manager to require**, all of your devices will have to follow the rules set in Configuration Manager.

System Security

These options are under the heading "System Security": Make mobile devices need a password to be unlocked: This one's for Windows and has to do with the PIN for Windows Hello for Business, not mobile devices.

- **Simple passwords**: Simple PINs like 1234 or 0000 will be blocked.
- **Password type**: It could be any of these:
  - **Device Default**: Password, PIN with numbers, or PIN with letters and numbers
  - **Numeric**: Only use a password or a PIN that is made up of numbers.
  - **Alphanumeric**: Password or alphanumeric only

To add some extra complication, the alphanumeric option is the one that should be chosen.

- **Minimum password length**: the number of digits for the PIN (make sure this is allowed by company policy and fits how you set up other PINs).
- **Maximum minutes of activity before password is required**: This can be anything from **Not Configured**, eight hours, or even one minute. It is suggested that you wait 15 minutes to find a good balance between security and user experience.
- **Password expiration**: How many days do users have to change their password before it expires (1–730)?

- **Number of previous passwords to prevent reuse**: How many times does a password have to be used before it can be used again?
- **Require password when device returns from idle state**: Only Windows Mobile and Holographic, require a password when the device comes back from being idle.

They won't force the settings to be used; instead, they'll just see if the device can handle them. The device would be marked as non-compliant if you did not configure any extra rules (Settings library and so on).

Encryption

Let us look at the settings under the Encryption heading:

- **Require encryption of data storage on device**: This security check is easier than the "Require BitLocker" option, but you don't have to restart your computer.

Device Security

The next section is called "Device Security," and it has the following settings:

- **Firewall**: Windows Firewall must be turned on and monitoring traffic
- **Trusted Platform Module (TPM):** Needs a TPM to be present (this is a requirement for installing Windows 11 anyway, so it only works on Windows 10 devices)
- **Antivirus:** Antivirus software must be present. This could be Windows Defender or a different program, as long as the Security Center has entered it and knows what it is. A custom compliance policy could give you more options if you're working with a third party.
- **Antispyware:** This is the same thing as antivirus, but it stops spyware.

Defender

Under "Defender," we can find the following settings:

- **Microsoft Defender antimalware**: Makes sure the antimalware service is turned on and working.
- **Microsoft Defender Antimalware minimum version**: The least amount of anti-malware software, like 4.11.0.0.
- **Microsoft Defender Antimalware security intelligence up-to-date**: Makes sure the signatures have been changed.
- **Real-time protection:** This check makes sure that the real-time protection service is turned on and running.

Microsoft Defender for Endpoint

Keep in mind that you will need to license Defender for Endpoint to use these settings. Before you turn this option on, make sure you have the right licenses:

Require the device to be at or under the machine risk score: The options are the following:

- **Not Configured**: No setting will be applied
- **Clear**: The device cannot have any threats at all
- **Low**: The device can only have low-level threats
- **Medium**: The device can have low or medium-level threats
- **High**: This allows all threat levels

How to do it...

We can make our policy now that we understand what each of the settings does. For this example, we'll keep things pretty simple, but you can change it to fit your needs:

1. To begin, go to **Devices** and then **Compliance**.
2. Go to Policies and click on **Create Policy**.
3. Use the drop-down menu to choose Windows 10 and later, then click Create.
4. We start with the **Name and Description** values and click Next, just like we do with any other policy or profile.
5. Using the information we went over earlier, we need to configure our settings now. We will need all of the Device Health options in this case, along with **Antivirus, Antimalware, Firewall,** and **TPM.**
6. Click **Next** after you've set it.
7. Now for the noncompliance actions. We already said that our device health rules need a restart, so we'll set that to 0.5 days. The machine that hasn't been seen in 180 days will be taken off the list of machines that need to be retired. Click Next after you have set up your environment.

NOTE: Adding a device to the retire list does not retire it; this is only for reporting.

8. Click Next because we don't want to set Scope tags.

NOTE: When looking at assignments for user-based devices, it's important to make sure that the policy is given to the right group of users. If the device is part of a device group, the policy will check both the user account and the system account for non-compliance. If either of them is found, the device will fail compliance.

9. Device-based assignments should only be used on tools that don't have users, like kiosks.
10. We are going to use the Intune-Users group. Click **Next** when you're done.
11. Finally, make sure everything looks good and click "**Create**."

A Windows compliance policy has now been set in the user interface.

Implementing an Android Compliance Policy

It's now time to look at our Android corporate devices. We don't have control over BYOD devices, so the App Protection policy handles them. However, we can make sure that controlled devices stay compliant so they can access corporate data. We will only be looking at devices that are owned and controlled by corporate here. We will start by looking at the options and what they do, just like we did with the Windows policy.

Compliance settings

Our Android devices have a lot of different compliance settings that we can go over.

Device Properties

We can change the following settings in Device Properties:

- Minimum and Maximum OS version: These are easy to understand. Don't forget that these are only for compliance and won't force a version or stop people from enrolling.
- Minimum security patch level: In the same way that Windows updates have security fixes and bigger operating system changes, so does Android. Usually, these come out once a month and you can set a minimum version requirement in a compliance policy. This could be helpful if there are any zero-day vulnerabilities. It needs to be in the form YYYY-MM-DD.

System Security

The following settings are in place for System Security:

- Require a password to unlock mobile devices: Remember that this won't make them use a password, and if you don't do anything about your non-compliant devices, they can keep using them without a password.
- **Required password type: The options are the following:**
    - **Device default**: It's not a good idea to do this because it can't be used to check for compliance.
    - **Password required, no restrictions**: Any password; you can't make any other restrictions.
    - **Numeric**: They can only be numbers. There is also the option for a minimum length (4–16).
    - **Numeric complex**: This type of complex can only have numbers and no patterns. There is also the option for a minimum length (4–16).
    - **Alphabetic**: Letters from the alphabet are the only ones that can be used. There is also the option for a minimum length (4–16).

- o **Alphanumeric**: Only capital letters, small letters, and numbers. There is also the option for a minimum length (4–16).
- o **Alphanumeric with symbols**: Uppercase and lowercase letters, numbers, punctuation marks, and symbols make up alphanumeric with symbols. This also shows the shortest password that can be (4–16 characters), the minimum number of characters that must be used (1–16), the minimum number of alphanumeric characters that must be used (1–16), the minimum number of non-letter characters that must be used (1–16), and the minimum number of symbol characters that must be used (1–16).
- **Maximum minutes of inactivity before password is required**: Find a good mix between security and ease of use here. It can be anywhere from one minute to eight hours.
- **Number of days until password expires**: This area is unnecessary. It shows the number of days until the password ends. The dates can be between 1 and 365 days, or they can be left blank to turn it off.
- **Number of passwords required before user can reuse a password**: This is also optional, and it can be set to any number between 1 and 24 if needed. Again, think about both the security effects and the possible user problems.

Device Security

Finally, we have a single setting under Device Security:

- **Intune app runtime integrity**: This makes sure that the default runtime environment is installed on Intune App (which used to be called Company Portal), that it is signed properly, and that it is not in debug mode.

How to do it...

We can set up the rules now that we understand how the settings work. This time, we'll set a few important things:

- To begin, go to **Devices** and click on **Android**.
- Click on **Compliance policies**.
- Click on **Create policy**.
- In the drop-down menu, choose **Android Enterprise** and then choose fully managed, dedicated, and corporate-owned work profile.
- After you've chosen these options, click **Create**.
- Type in a **Name** and a **Description**, and then click **Next**.
- **Make any necessary changes to the settings and click Next. We have set up the following in this example:**
  - o **Play Integrity Verdict**: Check the basic and device integrity
  - o **Required password type**: The password must be alphanumeric with symbols, six characters long, and include at least one of the available options.

- ○ **Require Encryption**

Now we need to set the noncompliance actions. Here are some extra choices that we will turn on since this is a mobile device. Once they're set up, click Next.

- In this case, we don't need scope tags, so click Next.
- Set your assignments. Like with Windows, it's best to set up machines that aren't kiosks with user-based assignments. You could use All Users and an Android filter instead of Intune users in this case. For different products, you might want to have different rules. After you've set your assignments, click "**Next**."
- Finally, make sure everything looks good and click **Create**.

In the UI, we have now set up our Android compliance policy.

Implementing an iOS Compliance Policy

- To begin, go to **Devices** and then **Compliance**.
- Go to **Policies** and click on **Create Policy**.
- Pick **iOS/iPadOS** from the drop-down menu and click **Create**.
- Type in the name and description of your policy, and then click **Next**.
- Change your settings as needed. In this case, we are blocking email that has been set up by the user and devices that have been hacked. We are also setting the password. After setting up your environment, click **Next**.
- Set the steps for non-compliant devices. Again, just like with Android, you can choose between emails and push alerts.
- In this case, we're not going to set any Scope tags, so click **Next**.
- For a better experience, we are using a user-based assignment once more. In this case, we are using the Intune-Users group we made. A lot of the time, your senior users will have iOS devices, so you may need different rules for each group of users. After making all the changes you want, click **Next**.
- Finally, check to make sure everything is right, and then click **Create**.

Implementing a macOS Compliance Protocol

- Begin by clicking **Devices** and then move on to **Compliance**.
- Go to **Policies** and click on **Create Policy**.
- Choose **macOS** from the drop-down menu and click "**Create**."
- Type in a **Name** and a **Description**, and then click **Next**.
- Make the necessary changes to the settings using the information above as a guide. After setting up, click **Next**.
- Set the steps for noncompliance. We can still lock the device from afar, but since this isn't iOS or Android, we can't send a push message.
- We're not setting any Scope tags in this case, as usual, so click **Next**.
- We've already talked about how giving to users gets better results, so we're doing that to our Intune-Users group.
- Finally, make sure everything is right, and then click **Create**.

Implementing a Linux Compliance Protocol

- Start by going to **Devices**, then **Compliance**.
- Go to **Policies** and click on **Create Policy**.
- Choose Linux from the drop-down menu in the fly-out. The bottom drop-down will then change to the Settings catalog. After that, click Create.
- Start with the **Name** and **Description** fields as normal, then click **Next**.
- Press **Add settings.**
- Add your settings as required. When you look at versions, first check the Ubuntu version URL to see which ones are still supported. Then, get rid of the ones that are no longer supported. We will only set a password in this area because we need encryption.
- When we choose "**non-compliance**," we can only email the person. Because the devices aren't managed, you can't retire them, and Linux doesn't work with push notifications. The restricted access policy will take care of the rest. For now, we will just mark it as non-compliant.
- As usual, we're going to skip over the Scope tags in this case, so click **Next**.
- Just like with other rules, we're giving them out at the user level. There is less of a risk of compliance with a Linux device, but coders and other IT staff may use them, so you may need to make some changes to your policies. Our Intune-Users Entra group is being used in this case. Click Next once you've chosen your task.
- Finally, check to make sure everything is right, then click **Create**.

How to configure and Implement a Windows custom compliance policy

You will occasionally discover that your compliance does not match what the built-in settings offer. For instance, you might need to keep an eye on third-party goods or block computers that have certain software loaded. For compliance, you could also limit your setting to a certain type of hardware, maker, and amount of RAM. PowerShell can find and use anything for compliance. As soon as the script is set up, you can use Intune to create a JSON policy that checks the PowerShell output against the settings and values we defined in the JSON. Being consistent means that the setting meets the expected value. If not, it is not compliant. One setting that is not compliant is enough to make a device work less well. We can set up our scripts now that we know how it works.

PowerShell script

Creating and sending our PowerShell script to Intune is the first step. To finish this, follow these steps:

- First, click on **Devices**. Next, click on **Compliance**.
- Now go to **Scripts**, click "**Add**," and pick **"Windows 10 and later."**

- Enter your Name and Description. You also have a Publisher field that you can change to your name or the name of your group if needed. After that, click **Next**.
- Paste your script into the box (you can't add files here). We haven't signed the script yet, so that should stay at No. Since we are asking for BIOS, we also want this to run at the system level. Lastly, 32-bit vs. 64-bit shouldn't matter for our questions, so it's best to leave it at Yes. After that, click Next.
- Now, make sure everything looks good, and then click Create.

Compliance policy

We can now create the policy with the script:

- Go to the **Policies** tab and click on **Create Policy**.
- Choose **Windows 10 or later** from the drop-down menu and click "**Create**."
- Type in the values for **Name** and **Description**, then click **Next**.
- We can now see the settings we talked about earlier. We are only setting Custom compliance this time.
- Click on "**Require**" under "**Custom compliance**," then click on the blue text that says Click to select to choose the script.
- Click **Select** after picking out your script from the list.
- Please choose your JSON. You will see that it fills in both the script (this box can only be read) and what it is looking for. If you think everything looks good, click **Next**.
- Set your non-compliance actions, then click **Next**.
- Since we're not setting any Scope tags here, click **Next**.
- As with other policies, we want to assign at the user level to keep things from going wrong. We're going to use Intune-Users in this case. When you're done setting up your assignment, click **Next**.
- The last step is to look over your policy and click **Create**.

That's all there is to setting up our custom Windows compliance policy in the UI.

Utilizing Conditional Access to Restrict Access According to Compliance

One more thing needs to be done before compliance policies can be used. We do have some non-compliance settings that lock down mobile devices, but most of the time we just let users know that their device isn't compliant, which doesn't stop them from using it. We don't want devices that don't meet our standards, like devices that aren't protected or that have malware running on them, to be able to view corporate data. To do that, we need to set up a strategy for conditional access policy. Make sure you have this breakglass account set up before we set up this policy. This way, we can keep it out of any limited access policies. This will let you get into the setting in case there is a problem with a policy that stops everyone else from getting in.

How to do it...

- To begin, go to Endpoint security and then Conditional access.
- Click Create a new policy.
- Give the policy a name and click on 0 users and groups selected.
- Pick All Users from the list under Include.
- Click the "Exclude" tab and exclude your Break Glass account. Think about your IT team. They might need to use these computers to get them back in line with the rules. We are going to add the Local Device Administrators job to the list of roles that are also not allowed in this case.
- Click on No target resources selected.
- These computers shouldn't be able to get to anything, so click **All cloud apps** under the **Include tab.**

Also, we don't want exclusion in this policy either. But when you're looking at future policies, you might want to exclude the Microsoft Intune Enrollment program if you want to allow device registration in situations where a conditional access policy would normally stop it, like when it's based on location. We need to be careful not to block personal devices that are not enrolled in MAM from using it because they will not comply because they are not enrolled in any way. It will be Device Based Filtering under Conditions that we use for this.

- Click **0 conditions selected** and then **Not configured** under **Filter for devices**.
- Change the rule to **DeviceOwnership Equals Company**. This will limit the policy so that it can only be used on devices owned by the corporate. To require app security on our BYOD devices, we made an extra policy here. Each of these policies adds another layer of protection on top of MFA, not instead of it. Click "**Done**":

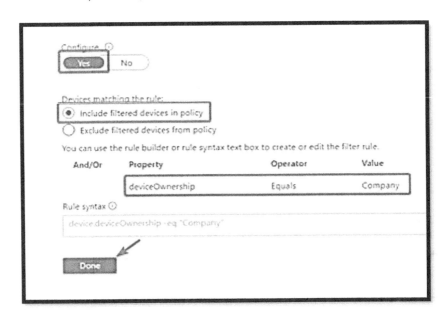

- Click **0 controls selected** under **Access controls**.
- Select **"Grant access"** because this is an "allow" policy instead of a "block" policy. Then, check the box next to **"Require device to be marked as compliant."**
- You can say whether the condition is any or all of the choices if you set more than one setting here. Once everything is set up, click Select.
- We don't need any controls over the session, so we can leave that choice unconfigured.

The last thing to think about is the policy's status, which changes depending on your environment. Setting this to On will result in calls to your IT support line because users won't be able to access corporate data if you have a lot of non-compliant devices. So, set it to "Report-only" and keep an eye on who will be blocked until you can fix the problem. Once most of your devices are following the rules, turn on the settings and add your security.

- We will turn on the policy in this case.

CHAPTER 9

INTEGRATION WITH MICROSOFT 365

Collaboration with Microsoft Teams

Microsoft Teams is where all of your team's information, people, and tools come together in Microsoft 365 so that they can work together better and be more involved. If you pay for the Enterprise Mobility + Security suite, which includes Microsoft Intune and Microsoft Entra ID P1 or P2 features like restricted access, you can protect your Microsoft 365 data in the most comprehensive and wide-ranging ways. You should set up at least a restricted access policy that lets mobile devices connect to Teams for iOS and Android and an Intune app security policy that keeps the teamwork experience safe.

Manage collaboration experiences in Teams for iOS and Android with Microsoft Intune

Apply Conditional Access

Companies can use Microsoft Entra Conditional Access policies to make sure that Teams for iOS and Android users can only view material that is related to work or school. You will need a restricted access policy that targets all possible users to do this. **Note**: The Microsoft Authenticator app needs to be loaded on iOS devices to use app-based restricted access policies. You need the Intune Company Portal app for Android devices.

Create Intune app protection policies

The App Protection Policies (APP) tells you which apps can use your company's data and what they can do with it. APP gives companies a lot of options so they can make the security fit their needs. Some people might not see which policy settings are needed to fully perform a scenario. Microsoft has added taxonomy to its APP data protection framework for iOS and Android mobile app management to help companies put mobile client endpoint safety at the top of their list of priorities. The APP data protection system is split into three separate setup levels. **Each level builds on the one before it:**

- **Enterprise basic data protection** (Level 1) makes sure that apps are private, protected with a PIN, and can be deleted selectively. This level makes sure that Android device authentication is correct for Android devices. This is an entry-level setup that gives you the same data protection controls as Exchange Online folder policies and lets IT and users get to know APP.

- **Enterprise-enhanced data protection** (Level 2) adds minimum OS needs and ways to stop app data leaks. This is the setting that most mobile users who receive work or school data will need.
- **Enterprise high data protection** (Level 3) adds advanced data protection features, better PIN setup, and APP Mobile Threat Defense. For users who are viewing high-risk material, this setup is best.

Whether the device is part of a unified endpoint management (UEM) system or not, you must create an Intune app security policy for both iOS and Android apps. The following factors must be met at the very least by these policies:

1. They include all Microsoft 365 mobile apps, like Edge, Outlook, OneDrive, Office, or Teams. This makes sure that users can safely access and change work or school data in any Microsoft app.
2. They're assigned to all users. This protects all users, whether they're on iOS or Android and use Teams.
3. Figure out which level of the structure meets your needs. Most businesses should use the settings in **Enterprise enhanced data protection** (Level 2) because they let them handle data protection and access standards.

Note: Users must also install the Intune Company Portal to protect apps on Android devices that aren't enrolled in Intune with Intune app protection policies.

Utilize app configuration

Teams for iOS and Android have app settings that let managers of unified endpoint management (like Microsoft Intune) change how the app works. The Managed App Configuration channel for iOS devices or the Enterprise channel for Android devices can be used to set up apps, or the Intune App Protection Policy (APP) channel can be used. Both of these channels can be used on enrolled devices.

The following configurations can be used with Teams for iOS and Android:

- Only allow work or school accounts

Each setup situation lists the specific needs that come with it. As an example, you should know if the setup situation needs Intune App Protection Policies or device enrollment, which means it can work with any UEM service. App configuration keys are case-sensitive. Make sure the setup works by using the right casing.

Note: A **Managed Devices** App Configuration Policy (ACP) is what Microsoft Intune calls app configuration sent through the MDM OS channel. A **Managed Apps** App Configuration Policy is what Microsoft Intune calls app configuration sent through the App Protection Policy channel.

Only allow work or school accounts

One of the most important parts of the Microsoft 365 value is that we follow the data security and compliance policies of our biggest and most controlled companies. Some companies have to keep track of all the talks that happen inside the company and make sure that the devices are only used for corporate communications. Teams for iOS and Android on enrolled devices can be set up so that only one company account can be created in the app. This is to meet these needs. This setup situation only works on devices that have been enrolled. Any UEM service is, however, fine. If you're not using Microsoft Intune, you should look at your UEM instructions to find out how to set up these setup keys.

Simplify the sign-in experience with domain-less sign-in

By setting the following policies, you can make it easier for people to sign in to Teams for iOS and Android by pre-filling the domain name on the sign-in screen for users on shared and controlled devices:

Name	Value
domain_name	A string value providing the domain of the tenant to appended. Use a semicolon delimited value to add multiple domains. This policy only works on enrolled devices.
enable_numeric_emp_id_keypad	A boolean value used to indicate that the employee ID is all numeric and the number keypad should be enabled for easy entry. If the value is not set, then the alphanumeric keyboard will open. This policy only works on enrolled devices.

Notification settings in Microsoft Teams

When you get notifications, you know what's going on or about to happen around you. Depending on how the settings are set, they show up on the home screen or the lock screen. To set up your alerts on the site through an app security policy, use the following choices.

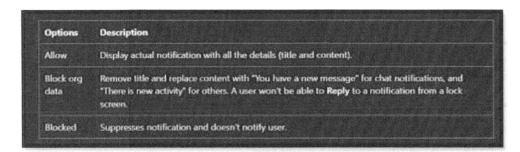

Options	Description
Allow	Display actual notification with all the details (title and content).
Block org data	Remove title and replace content with "You have a new message" for chat notifications, and "There is new activity" for others. A user won't be able to **Reply** to a notification from a lock screen.
Blocked	Suppresses notification and doesn't notify user.

For the notifications to show up on iOS and Android devices

1. Sign in to both Teams and Company Portal on the device. Set it to **Show Previews > Always** to make sure that your device's settings for alerts let Teams reach you.
2. Lock the device and let the person who is logged in on that device know about the message. You don't have to unlock the device to see a message when you tap on it on the lock screen.
3. **Notifications on the lock screen should look like this (screenshots are from iOS, but the same lines should show up on Android):**
   o You shouldn't be able to see the Reply or other quick response options for notifications from the lock screen.
   o You can't see the sender's image, but initials are fine.
   o The title of the notification should show up, but the text should say "You have a new message" for chat notifications and "There is new activity" for all other alerts.

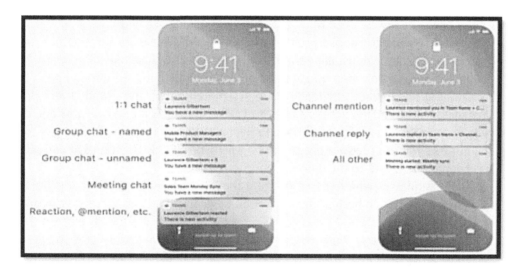

Integration with Office 365 apps

Add Microsoft 365 Apps to Windows 10/11 devices with Microsoft Intune

You have to add apps to Intune before you can give, watch, set up, or protect them. Microsoft 365 apps for Windows 10 and 11 devices are one type of app that can be used. If you choose this app type in Intune, you can give Windows 10 or 11 devices that you handle Microsoft 365 apps and install them. You can also give and set up apps for Microsoft Visio Online Plan 2 and Microsoft Project Online desktop software if you have the right licenses. In the Microsoft Intune control area, the list of apps shows the various Microsoft 365 apps as a single item.

Before you start

It's important to note that you must use the **Remove MSI** tool to safely remove any .msi Office apps that are on the end user's device. If not, the Microsoft 365 apps that Intune provided will not be able to be installed. When there is more than one necessary or open-app assignment, they don't add up. **A later app assignment will replace any loaded app assignments that are already there.**

- These apps can only be used on devices that have the Windows 10/11 Creators Update or later.
- You can only add Office apps from the Microsoft 365 Apps set to Intune.
- If any Office apps are open when Intune tries to install the app suite, it could fail, and users could lose data from files that haven't been saved yet.
- This way of installing won't work on devices that have Windows Home, Windows Team, Windows Holographic, or Windows Holographic for Business.
- If you have already installed Microsoft 365 apps to a device with Intune, you can't install Microsoft 365 desktop apps from the Microsoft Store. These are called Office Centennial apps. It's possible that installing this setup will damage or lose files.
- Multiple necessary or open-app assignments don't add up to more than one. A later app assignment will replace any loaded app assignments that are already there. Word, for instance, will be removed if the first set of Office apps has it and the later one does not. Any Visio or Project tool doesn't have to deal with this situation.
- Right now, you can't have more than one Microsoft 365 deployment. There will only be one deployment sent to the device.
- **Office version:** Pick whether to give them the 32-bit or 64-bit version of Office. A 32-bit version can be put on both 32-bit and 64-bit devices, but a 64-bit version can only be put on 64-bit devices.
- **Remove the MSI from end-user devices.** Choose whether you want to remove pre-existing Office .MSI apps from end-user devices. The installation won't succeed if there are pre-existing .MSI apps on end-user devices. The apps to be uninstalled aren't limited to the apps selected for installation in **Configure App Suite**, as it will remove all Office (MSI) apps from the end user device. When Intune reinstalls Office on your end user's machines, end users will automatically get the same language packs that they had with previous .MSI Office installations.

Select Microsoft 365 Apps

1. Go to the Microsoft Intune admin center and log in.
2. Select **Apps** > **All Apps**> **Add**.
3. Select **Windows 10 and later** in the **Microsoft 365 Apps** section of the **Select app type** pane.
4. Pick "**Select**." The steps for adding Microsoft 365 apps are shown.

Step 1 - App suite information

You give information about the app suite in this step. Users can find the app suite on the company site with the help of this information, which also aids in identifying the app suite in Intune.

1. **You can change or check the following values on the App suite information page:**
   - **Suite Name:** This is the name of the app suite that shows up on the company page. Make sure that each suite name you use is different. If there are two app suites with the same name, users will only see one of them on the company site.
   - **Suite Description**: Give the app suite a description. You could, for instance, make a list of the apps you've chosen to include.
   - **Publisher**: Microsoft appears as the publisher.
   - **Category**: You can choose one or more of the app's predefined groups or a category you create yourself. This setting helps users find the app suite faster when they look through the company portal or site.
   - **Show this as a featured app in the Company Portal**: Select this choice to make the app suite stand out when users are looking for apps on the main page of the company homepage.
   - **Information URL**: If you want to, you can enter the URL of a website that has information about this app. On the company site, the URL is shown to users.
   - **Privacy URL**: If you want to, you can put the URL of a website that has information about this app's privacy. On the company site, the URL is shown to users.
   - **Developer**: Microsoft appears as the developer.
   - **Owner**: Microsoft appears as the owner.
   - **Notes**: You can add any notes you want to link to this app under "Notes."
2. Click "**Next**" to see the **Configure app suite** page.

Step 2 - (Option 1) Configure app suite using the configuration designer

You can pick a template for changing app settings by choosing a Configuration settings format. Some choices for setting the format are:
- Configuration designer
- Enter XML data

In the Add app pane, when you choose Configuration Designer, there will be three more settings areas:
- Configure app suite
- App suite information
- Properties

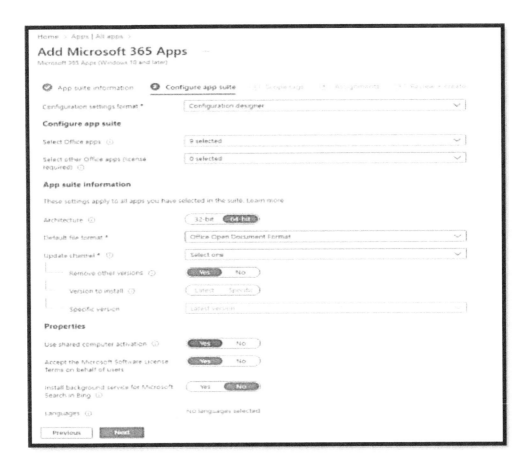

1. Go to the page for the **Configuration app suite** and pick out **Configuration Designer.**
- **Select Office apps**: By selecting the apps from the dropdown menu, select the standard Office apps that you want to give to devices.
- **Select other Office apps (license required)**: By selecting the apps from the dropdown list, you can give extra Office apps that you have rights for to devices. Some of these apps are paid ones, like Microsoft Project Online desktop client and Microsoft Visio Online Plan 2.
- **Architecture**: Decide whether to assign the 32-bit or 64-bit version of Microsoft 365 Apps. A 32-bit version can be put on both 32-bit and 64-bit devices, but a 64-bit version can only be put on 64-bit devices.
- **Default file format**: You can use **Office Open Document Format** or **Office Open XML Format** from the list.
- **Update Channel**: You can pick how your devices get updates for Office. Choose from:
  - Monthly
  - Monthly (Targeted)
  - Semi-Annual
  - Semi-Annual (Targeted)

After picking a channel, you can pick any of these options:

129

- Remove other versions: Users can get rid of other versions of Office (MSI) from their devices by clicking "Yes." Choose this option when you want to remove pre-existing Office .MSI apps from end-user devices. If they are already installed, the installation won't work on .MSI apps on devices used by end users. It won't just uninstall the apps chosen for download in Configure App Suite; it will also get rid of all Office (MSI) apps on the end user's device. When Intune reinstalls Office on the computers of your end users, the language packs they had before will be installed again.
- Version to install: Pick the version of Office that you want to set up.
- Specific version: If you chose Specific as the Version to install in the previous setting, you can choose to install a certain version of Office on end-user devices for the chosen channel.

The versions that are out there will change over time. Because of this, when you make a new deployment, the available versions may be newer and some older versions may not be. The older version will still be used in current deployments, but the list of versions will be updated all the time per channel. The reporting state for devices that update their pinned version (or any other features) and are published as ready will read "Installed" if they loaded the old version before the device check-in. It will briefly change to "Unknown" when the device checks in, but the person won't be able to see it. The state will change to "Installed" when the user starts the installation of the newer version.

- **Use shared computer activation**: Select this choice when multiple users are sharing a computer.
- **Automatically accept the app end user license agreement**: Select this choice if you don't want end users to have to agree to the license agreement. After that, Intune immediately agrees to the terms.
- **Languages:** Office is loaded automatically in any approved language that is on the device that the end-user has Windows on. Select this choice if you want to add more languages to the app suite.

For Microsoft 365 apps that are controlled by Intune, you can deploy more languages. The Type of language pack (core, partial, and proofing) is shown next to each language on the list. Go to the interface and click on **Microsoft Intune** > **Apps** > **All apps** > **Add**. In the Add app pane, search for "Windows 10 and later" and then choose it from the list of App types. Select **Languages** from the **App Suite Settings** pane.

2. Click **Next** to see the **Scope Tags** page appear.

Step 2 - (Option 2) Configure app suite using XML data

You can use a custom setup file to set up the Office app suite if you choose the **Enter XML data** choice from the **Setting format** dropdown box on the **Configure app suite** page.

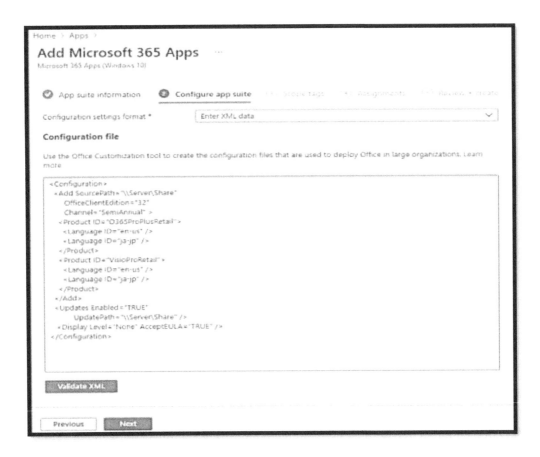

1. Put in your configuration XML.

Keep in mind that the Product ID can be Business (O365BusinessRetail) or Proplus (O365ProPlusRetail). But you can only use XML data to set up the Microsoft 365 Apps for Business version app package. Keep in mind that **Microsoft 365 Apps for Enterprise** is now called Microsoft Office 365 ProPlus.

2. Click **Next** to see the **Scope Tags** page appear.

Step 3 - Select scope tags (optional)

You can choose who can see information about client apps in Intune with scope tags.

1. If you want to add scope tags for the app suite, click **Select scope tags.**
2. Click **Next** to see the page with your assignments.

Step 4 - Assignments

1. Select the group assignments for the app suite that are **Required, Available for enrolled devices, or uninstall.**
2. Click "**Next**" to see the "**Review + create**" page.

Step 5 - Review + create

1. Go back and look over the app suite's values and settings.
2. Click **Create** to add the app to Intune when you're done.

The **Overview** blade is shown.

Deployment details

When the Intune deployment policy is applied to the target computers through the Office Configuration Service Provider (CSP), the end device will download the installation package from *officecdn.microsoft.com*. **In the Program Files directory, two new directories will appear:**

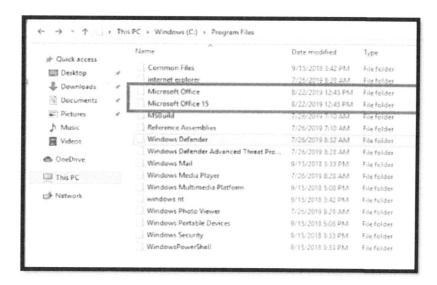

These files are kept in a new folder that is made under the Microsoft Office directory:

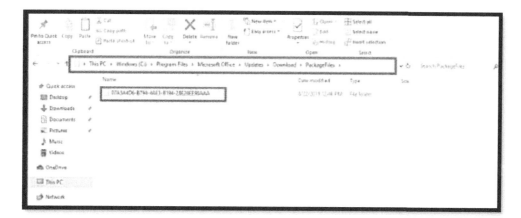

The files that start the Office Click-to-Run download are kept in the Microsoft Office 15 directory. If the assignment type is needed, the installation will begin itself:

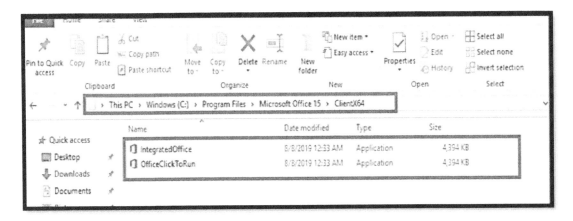

If the Microsoft 365 assignment is set up correctly, the update will run in quiet mode. Once the installation is done, the saved software files will be removed. As long as the assignment is set to "Available," the Office apps will show up in the Company Portal app so that end users can directly install them.

CHAPTER 10
WATCHING OUT YOUR NEW SETTING

One of the best things about current device management is that a properly set up system can free up staff time to be more proactive and find and fix problems before end users do.

Monitoring Applications

We will begin by looking at monitoring application licenses. Next, we will go through the other features in the order that they show up in Intune:

App licenses

App licenses are the first thing on our menu. Only store-based apps (Apple, Microsoft, and Google Play Store) can use this. For each program, you choose how many licenses to make available when you use Apple Volume Purchase to install it. If your apps are free, you can order as many as you need, but if they cost money, you might want to limit the licenses. Any app will stop releasing when its license limit is reached, so keeping an eye on how licenses are being used is a good idea. At the top, you can add more columns (most of which will have no data), refresh, export to CSV, and, most importantly, start a VPP sync. When you click on the three dots, you can also delete the app, which can be helpful. The apps are given in alphabetical order, and there is no way to change that. However, you can use the free text field at the top to narrow down the list. If you want to sort, which is much more useful, check out the automation? It uses the Out-GridView command to give you a similar screen but with more control. Once you click on an application, you will be taken to information about that application.

Discovered apps

Discovered apps are the next item on the menu. This report is for all applications and has a list of all the apps that can be found on devices that are controlled by Intune, whether they were installed by Intune or not. It is a strong tool, but because each version is its record, it can be hard to keep track of (a small tenant could have more than 1,000 entries). We can export using the button at the top, search, and look through, but there is no way to sort. When you click on an app, you'll be taken to a page with more information about that app, where you can see more install reports. Like app licenses, the script will let you sort things in more ways.

App install status

This is the next item on the list: the **App installs status** choice for all apps on all devices. Like with all of Intune's other reports, you can Filter, Search, and Export this one. Of course, this blade also lets you sort by the columns, which is a nice touch. The app name will take you to the main page with information about the app. If you click on **Device failures or User failures**, you will go straight to the **Device install status** or **User install status** page. Look at this often to find any apps that are giving you trouble or coming in the wrong package before you start getting support calls. You can get the best idea of what is wrong with your estate by sorting by Install failure. This will show you both device and user installations that failed.

App Protection status

One important thing for any security team to do is check the state of protected apps on both personal and corporate devices. You can export, search, and sort on the headers, just like in App install status. You can see that there are many columns here, so keep an eye on the scroll bar at the bottom. The most important fields, like **App protection status** and **Compliance state,** are near the bottom. Since these are MAM devices, there is no more click through. Monitoring your app protection state will help you figure out what's wrong when users are blocked from resources, while conditional access will keep your business data safe.

App Configuration Status

App Configuration Status is the last report for monitoring a program. This is for any application setup policies you've put in place for managed devices or managed apps (MDM and MAM). It works for both Android and iOS devices at the device level. Just like with other reports, you can search, refresh, and export this one. One more thing it lets you do is sort by header. Again, there is a lot of information here, so use the menu. Luckily, most of the important settings are near the beginning. This usually won't have any major security problems, but it's still worth keeping an eye on for the best user experience.

Tracking Device configuration

We can now look at watching the devices themselves, starting with the configuration profiles that are used on them, since we know how to track our apps. At this point, the **New Devices Experience** view is in test and can be used by choosing to do so. This will likely become the default, so we only used the New Devices Experience view. Click on **Devices**, then **Overview**, and then click the words at the top:

For setting up a device, there are three monitoring choices that we will go over one at a time. To find them, go to Manage Devices and click on Devices. Then, click on Configuration. After that, you'll be taken to the Monitor tab in the new version, where you can find our choices, which we will now go over.

Devices with restricted apps

Any **device restriction** policies across OS systems will work with this choice. You can set up a strategy to block certain apps, and any device that is found to have these apps will be marked in the report. In this case, we have set up a macOS restriction profile to stop people from using **Apple Calculator (so that it works):**

In the monitoring result, the device is marked as having an app that isn't allowed (prohibited):

The apps that have been found will be shown when you click on the row. At the top, there is the standard Export button, a search function (though it only looks for the user's email address), and a useful sorting function based on column names.

Encryption report

This is an important one to keep an eye on, but hopefully, your well-thought-out compliance policies and Conditional Access will protect you at least some. That keeps these devices from getting to M365 data, but there is still a risk if an unsecured device with files saved locally is lost or stolen. Monitoring your devices that aren't encrypted is therefore a very important job. Keep in mind that this only works for Windows and macOS devices, so don't expect to see any Android or iOS ones there. It's annoying that you can't sort by column titles and that you can only look by device or username. This makes it harder to find your unsecured devices in a big setting; instead, use the script in the automation section. You can narrow down the results, though, by pressing the filter button at the top. **Readiness** is a useful header that will quickly let you know if a device isn't secured and whether the problem is with the policy or the device itself. The device should not be used remotely if the **Trusted Platform Module (TPM)** is not operational and the device is not ready. Instead, a hands-on look at the hardware is recommended. We can now proceed to our next report, which is about monitoring certificates.

Certificates

Certificates are the last monitoring choice for device setup. This is only important if you are using Intune to push certificates to your devices for things like login, app packaging, and so on. Again, the two most important headings are right at the end: **Certificate expiry and Certificate status.** If you are on a smaller screen, you may want to press the Columns button to get rid of some headings you don't need or drag to change their order. You can export and sort by column heading, and search (including free text), but you will find that the filter button has been taken away. For general tracking, you should sort by expiration. If you need to find something more quickly, you can use the search function. We can move on to the secret assignment fails to report after we look over our certificates.

Assignment failures

There is one more monitoring choice that isn't mentioned in the other three: assignment **failures.** This option looks at failures at the policy level when you look at the device setup. To get to this, go to **Devices** and click on the blue text that says **"Configuration profile status."** This will bring up a new screen where you can quickly check to see which of your policies are wrong or don't work right on all of your devices. You can sort by column headers to quickly find policies that have failed in a big way. You can also look by profile name. You can also use a more complex filter to limit by device, profile type, or profile source. Should you click on the profile name, you will be taken to a different screen where you can see which devices are having trouble with the profiles. This report would be clear in a perfect world, but there will always be problems on different devices. Start by looking at devices that are in conflict. These are not device faults, but policy configuration or scoping faults, which means that you have two policies that are at odds with each other on the same device. Keep in mind that a policy can be at odds with itself even if all of its settings are the same. After getting rid of the policies that don't work together, you can move on to the mistakes. If the value is more than a third of your total estate, it's usually a problem with the insurance (if you have a bigger estate). Not the device.

Tracking Device Compliance

After keeping an eye on device configuration, we also need to keep an eye on device compliance. This is especially important because once users are limited to non-compliant devices; this will be the most frustrating issue. Click on **Devices** and then **Compliance** to get to these reports. The next step will take you to the **Monitor tab**, where you can see the next six reports. We will start by looking at non-compliant devices, and then we will go through the other reports that are out there.

Noncompliant devices

This report starts with noncompliant devices. It shows all devices, on all systems (including Linux), that don't follow any compliance strategy. One failure will put all of a device's policies out of compliance if it has more than one. To look for a device name, device ID, login, user email, user ID, IMEI, or serial number, you can use the search function. The usual sections and Export button are also there. You can sort by the headings or filter by **Compliance status, OS, Ownership type, and Device type.** If you click on a device, you will be taken to a page with more information about that device instead of the Device compliance panel itself. If you have Conditional Access set to block non-compliant devices, you should keep an eye on this one so you can fix problems before the user gets blocked and calls to report.

Devices without compliance policy

This is another simple one that will show you any devices that don't have any policies applied to them. If you set up the general settings properly, this will mark the devices as non-compliant right away, which will help you figure out what's wrong. Checking here is even more crucial if you have the setting to mark them as compliant to ensure that all of your devices are properly protected and watched. It only lets you export, choose columns (which can't be sorted), and do a search at the time this was written. There are, however, plans for the future to make things better.

Setting compliance

This monitoring choice checks the settings that are in place for all of your compliance policies, even the ones that aren't built by Microsoft. On top of the original list of devices that didn't follow the rules, it tells you exactly which settings in the policies are making the devices not follow the rules. If this is your first start, you may need to click the **Sync report** button at the top to sync the results. The information that is shown can be exported, and the headers can be used to find or sort. Any click on any of the rows will bring up more information, such as the devices that aren't compatible because of the setting. Ordering by non-compliant devices will help you quickly figure out if the problem is with a setting or with an individual device. The **Is active setting** is based on the time in the Compliance settings. Depending on the value you have set, it may be near the top of groups.

Policy compliance

By now, we can see both non-compliant devices and the settings that are making them non-compliant. However, this only tells us about the settings themselves, not the policy they are part of. We have a choice called "**Policy compliance**" that shows each compliance policy and the number of devices that are compliant, non-compliant, or in an error state. Again, you can do a first syncing of the report when you view it for the first time. You can download the data, search, and sort the titles after it's done. Compliant devices shouldn't be a problem, so the best way to deal with this is to sort by non-compliance and mistakes. When you click on the name of a policy, you will be taken to a page that lists all the devices that are in line with that policy.

Noncompliant policies

At the time of writing, this is still in test and is pretty much the same as the last choice. The only difference is that it doesn't list anything compliant, so it only shows things that aren't compliant or are wrong. It shows all kinds of devices and lets you sort them by platform. You can also look by policy name, export, and sort by heading, as usual. When you click on a policy, you'll be taken to a list that only shows the devices that are having problems, not all of them like the last option did. For day-to-day management, this choice is better than the last one because it cuts down on the amount of data and lets you focus on the parts you need to see.

Windows health attestation report

The last choice for monitoring device compliance is the Windows health attestation report. This report only works on Windows and looks at how the device's attestation settings are set up. This can be used to quickly see if there are any problems with the hardware or software that might put BitLocker or Secure Boot at risk. Pay attention to the toolbar at the bottom of the screen. You can also use the Columns button to get rid of any areas that don't apply to your situation. **The result is pretty easy. Although there is no search function or way to sort by headers, there is a filter that can be used:**

Since you can't click on any of the results, you can only look at it here.

Monitoring Device Enrollment

We can now check that our devices are compliant and set up correctly, but that won't help if they haven't enrolled. That is why we need to use the choices for device registration and tracking. When users are self-enrolling devices, these are especially helpful for looking for mistakes and helping with fixing them. Click on **Devices** and then **Enrollment** to get to these reports. This will bring you to the Monitor panel, where you can see our choices, which we will now go over in more depth. First, we will look at failed enrollments. Then, we will go through each report that is provided.

Enrollment failures

First, we look at enrollment failures, which is a report that shows all failed enrollments across all platforms and any approved signup method. It also has information about errors, which is very helpful. The strong filter here should be the first thing you look at. It can look at the platform, mistake type, registration type, and date and time of the entry. This will make it much easier to find any spikes or fails that happen repeatedly. Another option is to export the results as a CSV file. One more thing that is unique to this choice is that you can choose to show for All users or just one person (Select user). This is a very helpful tool for users who are having trouble enrolling. Not only can you not sort by name, but the strong filter should make that unnecessary. You can also see a graph, which is helpful for regularly checking for any sudden drops in enrollment failures that might be caused by a change in the firewall or a power loss somewhere.

Incomplete user enrollments

This section is only for Android and iOS devices that were enrolled through the Company Portal. It does not cover Android for Work, Zero Touch, or Apple Business Manager Enrollments. It shows a graph of enrollments that the user did not finish, either because they closed the enrollment screen or the enrollment timed out. This should be empty by default, but it's worth keeping an eye on it so you can help any users on the list. Another strong filter is at the top. It lets you sort by operating system, date/time, or the stage of registration at the time of cancellation/timeout.

Windows Autopilot deployments

The last choice only works on Windows devices and shows a list of all successful and unsuccessful Autopilot launches from the last 30 days. It has another strong filter, just like the other reports we looked at. You can find and sort by name, but not download data. For that, you will need to use automation. When you click on a device, the Autopilot device information will appear. Monitoring these events is always helpful because Autopilot is usually set up by the user. The last thing you want is to deploy a device that isn't fully set up yet. You can also look at the overall time to see how the person is doing and if there is anything that could be done to make it better.

Monitoring Updates across Platforms

Keeping your devices up to date with the latest security changes is a must in most settings. Sometimes devices will have trouble getting updates, even though Intune has tools that can do it for you. To check these, we can see if there are any updates for Windows, iOS, and macOS (but not yet for Android). We need to go to Devices in the Intune menu to get to these reports. Each one is in a different place, which will be talked about in its report. We will start this section by talking about updates for Windows. Then we will talk about updates for iOS and macOS.

Windows updates

Click on Windows 10 and later updates in Devices. After that, this gives you a general idea of the following:

- **Update ring device status**: This shows which devices are having problems with the update ring policies as a whole, not just with one version.
- **Feature update device errors**: This shows you how many devices in your policies are having trouble deploying feature updates.
- **Expedited update failures**: The same thing as before, but for updates that happen quickly. You should keep a close eye on this one because quick updates are usually for important security problems.
- **Driver update failures**: This will show you any devices whose drivers have failed if driver updates are turned on.

On any of the reports, clicking on the three dots in the upper right corner will take you to the report below:

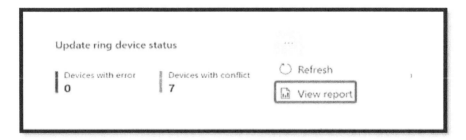

Then, you can click on rows in the report to get more information if you need to. There is a choice to export your info in the report. Use the main page to get a basic idea of the land, and then use the individual reports to figure out what's wrong and fix it. Do not start with policy mistakes. If a policy is not being applied to a device, it might not be getting any updates. After they are fixed, the next most important thing to look at is faster updates.

iOS update status

You can access this choice by going to **Devices** and then **Apple Updates**. Finally, click on the iOS update status. You will see a style that you are used to seeing here, along with a list of your iOS devices that can't be installed. Apple doesn't report on devices that are working fine, so it will only show the ones that have problems. Not only can you download, but there is also a strong filter that can look at both a range of dates and the installation status.

Here is a full list of all the options:

You can sort the headers and there is also a free-text search. There are a lot of things that could go wrong with an update, like getting a call, so this is always something to keep an eye on, especially since C-level executives often use iOS devices.

macOS update status

Devices | Apple Updates | macOS Update Status is where you can find this one. When we click on it, we're taken to a different report screen that looks a lot like the iOS screen but has a few fewer features. The filter lets you set the minimum and maximum OS versions, but it also limits the update status choices. There is the standard **Export** button and a search box that looks through the main things. However, you can't click on the headers and sort them. There isn't as much information here as there is for Windows and iOS, but there is enough to find devices that aren't working right and fix them.

Monitoring Device Activities

As an Intune supervisor, especially in a bigger company, you need to keep track of who did what because there are buttons in the panel that can do bad things. Let's say someone clicks "Wipe" on the wrong device by accident, and you need to write up an incident report about what happened. These are all logged Device actions, which is good news. Go to **Devices**, then **Overview**, and finally click on the Device Actions box to get to these logs. This screen will show you a list of all the actions that were taken on all devices, including what was done when it was done, and who did it. You can't search or sort by labels (you'll need to use the automatic script to do that), but it does have a powerful filter that includes all actions that can be taken on any device:

It can only be viewed (or exported if you click the **Export** button). You can't drill down with this tool. You should only have to fill out this report very rarely but think of it as your insurance policy.

Examining Audit Logs

In the last section, we talked about monitoring actions that are made directly on devices. These actions can have a big effect, but they only affect one device at a time, so they are less likely to cause big problems. The likelihood of problems on a bigger scale increases significantly if policies are changed, removed, or made. We need to look through the audit logs to keep an eye out for these kinds of changes. You will see a screen that looks like a report once you get to the Audit Logs page. Again, there is a strong filter option at the top that lets you do things like sort by activity. But keep in mind that this is a big list that doesn't have a built-in search function, so make sure you make the right choice when you use it. In the search box, you can find the person who made the change. You can also sort by date and activity, but not by any of the other headers. If you click "Export," this will only send what's on the screen and not any other information you can grab. When you click on a row, you can see more details about what was changed, such as the new and old values. This is very helpful if you need to undo a change but don't have a record of the old value (or use a backup/restore tool).

CHAPTER 11

ABOUT POWERSHELL SCRIPTING ACROSS INTUNE

A useful feature of Intune that isn't always noticed is its scripting engine. Scripts can be run on devices either one time (Platform scripts) or constantly (Remediations, which used to be called Proactive Remediations). Along with Windows 10 and 11, PowerShell has gotten so powerful that devices can now do almost anything with a script. We can use PowerShell scripts in Intune to set features that aren't yet in the settings library, copy files, add registry keys, or even run a script to get rid of unnecessary Windows junk for a better build. As setups, platform scripts are run to make easy configuration settings or do anything else that needs to be done during device setup. On the other hand, remediations are scripts that can be run again and again, but their reasoning only runs when it's needed. We will not only learn how to use PowerShell scripts and Remediations but also how to write them and give you some sample scripts to get you started. This will cover not only fixes and platform scripts but also the use of scripts in deploying applications.

Platform Scripts Deployment

We will begin with the first choice, which has been in Intune longer than the others. Platform scripts only need to be run once on the device. They can be run as the system or as a user. When they are first deployed, they run in 32-bit mode, but this can be changed. This is important to remember because the settings will be different for system/user and 32/64-bit. When Autopilot is running, scripts run when it says "Preparing apps" in the User or Device setup. There is no name for this step. It's possible that a PowerShell script failed and didn't report a success code in time if you run into this time-out problem. Get the script ID from the address bar in the Intune site to look at the results of a script and figure out what went wrong. The output will be in the following place, under a subkey that has the ID:

- *HKLM:\Software\Microsoft\IntuneManagementExtensio n\Policies*

Logging should be built into the script itself so that the output is more complete and easier to find.

Getting started

We will use a simple script to deploy a registry key and get rid of a built-in Windows AppX app in this case. **Create a new PowerShell script in your preferred editor, then type the following code into it:**

Get-AppxPackage -allusers -Name
Microsoft.BingNews| Remove-AppxPackage -AllUsers
$Search =
"HKLM:\SOFTWARE\Policies\Microsoft\Windows\Window
s Search"

```
If (!(Test-Path $Search)) { New-Item $Search
}
If (Test-Path $Search) {
Set-ItemProperty $Search AllowCortana -Value
0
}
```

This will remove Bing News and prevent Cortana from appearing in the search box.

Once you've written your script, do these things to deploy it:

- Go to **Devices** in the Intune gateway, click on **Windows**, and then click on **Scripts and Remediations.**
- If nothing else is chosen, you will be taken to **Remediations**. At the top, click on the **Platform Scripts** tab. Then, click on **Add.**
- As always, give your script a **Name** and a **Description**. You will not be able to see the script's content in the gateway after adding it, but you can download and decode it through **Graph** if you need to. Because of this, it is important to be careful in your comments and keep a copy of the source files. After you've set these up, click Next.
- *On the first page of script settings, choose the script you added. After that, we have a few choices:*
  - **Run this script using the logged-on credentials**: This can be set to Yes to run the scripts in the user's context and let them get to the user's data. Your users can't do anything else, though, unless they have administrative rights.
  - **Enforce script signature check**: If you set this to "Yes," the script will only run if it has the right signature. This should usually be set to No for scripts that you make yourself. To keep things safe, make sure you sign each script before you share it.
  - **Run script in 64-bit PowerShell host:** If you don't change this, any registry keys you write will go to WOW6432Node and files will go to Program Files (x86). If you change this to "Yes," the script files and results will be written in the main places.
- For the last script to work, it needs to run at the System level and in a 64-bit host because it is writing to HKEY Local Machine (HKLM). Since our script isn't signed, the signature check setting needs to be set to "No":

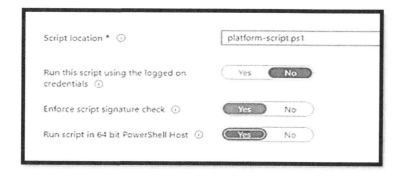

- Once everything is set up, click **Next.**

- We don't need Scope tags for this, so click **Next** once more.

Putting the script in place is now the next step. To make it run during the Device phase of Autopilot, send it to a device group. To make it run during the User phase, send it to a user group. In this case, the script is to clean the device, so we will run it in the device context to be sure it is done before a person logs in. After setting up, click Next.

- Last, make sure all of your settings are correct on the **Review + Add screen**, then click **Add**.

Your PowerShell Platform Script is now made, uploaded, and added to Intune.

Getting Started with Configuring Remediations

Platform scripts are great for cases where you only want to run something once, like when you're setting up a device. However, PowerShell is very powerful, and you may want to run something more than once or see the results in the shell. This is where Remediations (which used to be called Proactive Remediations) come in. You can set them to run at a certain time, but because they work with a monitoring and remediation setup, the script will only run if it needs to. Remediation has two scripts: one for detection and one for Remediation. The detecting script may be more important than the remediation script because it tells the remediation script whether it needs to run or not. This key gives out the exit code. The device is compliant with the check if the exit code is 0, so no additional action is required. When the exit code is 1, the remediation starts. You can put anything you want in the scripts as long as the two exit codes are set. We will add a Remediation to this method that should work well in most situations and clean up the disk if it gets low on space.

We must first create two scripts, one for detection and the other for remediation. Create the following PowerShell scripts using the tool of your choice:

Detect.ps1:

$storageThreshold = 15

$utilization = (Get-PSDrive | Where {$_ .name - eq "C"}).free

*if(($storageThreshold *1GB) -lt $utilization){ write-output "Storage is fine, no remediation needed"*

exit 0}

else{

write-output "Storage is low, remediation needed"

exit 1}

Remediate.ps1:

$cleanupTypeSelection = 'Temporary Sync Files', 'Downloaded Program Files', 'Memory Dump Files', 'Recycle Bin'

foreach ($keyName in $cleanupTypeSelection) {

$newItemParams = @{

Path   =

"HKLM:\SOFTWARE\Microsoft\Windows\CurrentVersi

on\Explorer\VolumeCaches\$keyName"

```
Name    = ‹StateFlags0001›
Value   = 1
PropertyType    =       'DWord'
ErrorAction     =       ‹SilentlyContinue'
}       @newItemParams | Out-Null
New-ItemProperty
}
Start-Process -FilePath CleanMgr.exe -
ArgumentList '/sagerun:1' -NoNewWindow -Wait
```

The detection script only checks the C drive for free room. It sends **Exit code 0** if it is less than 15 GB, which starts the remediation. The data that is sent with the exit code is another thing to think about. The detection output can be seen in the Intune dashboard after it has been run, so adding useful write-output will help you later when you want to check on the device's status. Following the remediation, the disk cleanup tool is used to get rid of temporary files, downloaded programs, memory dump files, and the trash bin (as needed). The remediation script doesn't need an exit code.

How to do it…

Create your scripts now, and then add them to Intune by following these instructions:

To get to **Scripts and remediations**, go to **Devices** and click on **Windows**. It will start with "Remediations" at the top, so click "**Create**." Add the **Name** and **Description** values, just like in the last section. You can also add an author here; the log-in user's name will appear automatically, but it's a blank field. It is a good idea to add a good description, but if necessary, remediations can be seen in the site after they have been added. After setting up, click Next. There are screens where you can add your Detection and Remediation scripts. You can set the context in the same ways you can with PowerShell scripts: 32-bit or 64-bit, system, and signing. We need system context, 64-bit, and unsigned in this case. After setting up, click Next:

For a site-wide remediation like this, Scope tags are not necessary, so click **Next**. Now, give the Remediation the job it requires. It will show you that you can also add All Users or All Devices. After picking your group, click the "Daily" text. This will bring up a menu where you can choose when the remediation should run. You can choose between **Daily** (where you can choose how many days and what time), **Hourly**, and Once (with a set date and time). The detecting script won't greatly affect the devices in this case, so we'll run it every hour.

After setting up, click Next:

Last, make sure everything looks good, then click Create. You will see that Version is written as "No Version." On the first screen, there was a text box that could not be changed. It will keep going up as you make changes to the scripts. Now that our remediation is on the site, we can look into scripting it so that we can quickly put in place new scripts.

There is more...

According to what was already said, remediations give us some extra features besides timing that Platform scripts don't have. Let us take a look.

Viewing output

You can view the script's results in the shell instead of having to go to the device itself. This is a secret but very useful function.

Here are the steps you need to take:

To get to the Scripts and Remediations page in the Intune interface, go to Devices and then Windows. Click Scripts and Remediations. Click on the script you want to go to in your list of scripts. Now, go to the left menu and click on Monitor. Then, click on Device status. If you click on Columns, you will see more choices. The normal status is cut down so that it fits on the screen.

Check the boxes next to the **Pre-remediation detection output** and **post-remediation detection output**, then click **Apply**:

The results from the detecting script will now be shown, both before and after remediation. If you set write-output to something in your recognition script, this result will only be as good as that. This is something you should think about when writing your scripts. We can look at running remediations whenever we want now that we know how to see the results.

Running remediations on demand

Run remediations on demand is another useful tool that can help you if you need to do one fast. This is very helpful for quick security fixes or when you are trying to figure out what's wrong with a device. In the detecting script, you could list any common mistakes so that you know where to start. Then, you could run a remediation with standard steps for fixing problems.

This is what you need to do to run remediation on demand on a device:

- To start it whenever you want, go to **Devices**, click on **Windows**, and then click on your device from the list.
- Now, click the three dots (...) and choose Run remediation.

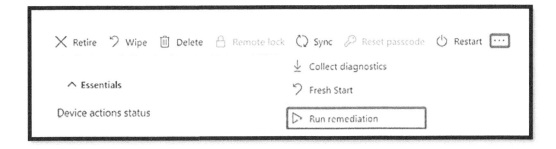

You will see a list of deployed remediations in the tenancy. Click **Run remediation** after selecting the one you want to run (you can only pick one). Through Graph, you can do a remediation on many devices at the same time.

Utilizing Custom Detection Scripts in Applications

When you make your detection script, remember that it needs both an **exit code (0)** and a **standard output (STDOUT).** If you send an exit code of 1 or leave out the STDOUT, the installation will be marked as failed.

The script needs to send something out before it can search the STDOUT. That's why the following code will work and mark the installation as complete:

Write-output "App found"
Exit 0
Finally, we can use and put into action a unique detection script:
- Whether you add the script during packaging or after deployment, you need to do so to use a custom detection script. To get to post-deployment, go to Apps and then Windows. Click on the app in question when you find it.
- Now, go to **Properties** and click on **Edit** next to **Detection rules**.
- Choose **"Use a custom detection script"** from the dropdown menu, and then navigate to the detection script you made.

NOTE: You can't choose between system and user context. One annoying thing about this is that custom detection scripts only run in the system context, even when the app is running at the user level. You will need to use your script to find the currently logged-in user and add that user to **c:\users\ or HKCU** to access files or registry keys in the user context. The GitHub project has a method that will return the SID and username of the currently logged-in person.

- Choose the right 32-bit or 64-bit settings. This is very important for programs because you will often be looking for registry keys or files in the **Program Files** area. You need to make sure that the script asks for the right place.
- Finally, turn on or off the **Enforce script signature check and run script silently**. Set this to No if your scripts are not signed. You don't need to worry about the part that says "run script silently." Unsigned scripts will also run in the background while they take over the system.
- Once everything is set up, click **Review + Save.**
- Finally, make sure everything looks good and click **"Save."**

That's all there is to this recipe for using and putting in place a custom detection script. We can now look at some cases from real life.

Examples of application detection scripts

Here are a few examples to give you an idea of how app detection scripts work. It is often easier to fully understand the output needs when you can see a script that is already running:

This script will easily check the 7-Zip data:

```
$Path = "HKLM:\SOFTWARE\7-Zip"
$Name = "Path"
$Type = "STRING"
$Value = "C:\Program Files\7-Zip\"
Try {
$Registry = Get-ItemProperty -Path $Path - Name $Name -ErrorAction Stop | Select-Object - ExpandProperty $Name
If ($Registry -eq $Value)
{ Write-Output "Detected" Exit 0}
Exit 1}
Catch {Exit 1}
```

This script uses file detection for the following app:

```
$File = "C:\windows\system32\notepad.exe"
if (Test-Path $File) {
write-output "Notepad detected, exiting"
exit 0
}
else {
exit 1
}
```

TIP: In real life, you would probably use the GUI tools to make these kinds of discoveries, so we will talk about some uses that go beyond that.

This example script will verify that a service has been built and is active. If your app won't run without a service, this will help:

```
$service = get-service -name "MozillaMaintenance"
if ($service.Status -eq "Running") { write-output "MozillaMaintenance detected
and running, exiting"
exit 0
}
else {
exit 1
}
```

You can find out when the file was last changed if you want to be sure you have the most recent version but don't trust the application's provider versioning:

```
$filedate = (Get-Item
"C:\Windows\System32\notepad.exe").LastWriteTi
me
if ($filedate -gt (Get-Date).AddDays(-1)) { write-output "Detected"
exit 0
}
else {
exit 1
}
```

Using the UI and some samples, that concludes setting detection scripts. Let's now look at how to make this process automatic.

Utilizing Custom Requirements Scripts in Applications

You can also use custom needs scripts with PowerShell. The necessary rules cover a lot of ground, but you might want to go even further. For example, you could say that an app can only be used on a device made by a certain company. One time these are especially useful is when you are updating apps that are already installed. Since these were installed by the user, when you push an update to them, the user has to download and install the current version from the business site (as long as the rules are set up properly to know it needs to be reinstalled). This is not a good idea at all, especially when you have a zero-day hack. In this case, you can give everyone the app they need and then set a rule that says it has to check to see if the app is already on the device before installing it. These don't work like remediation or detection scripts; instead, they're more like **compliance scripts**. We don't need an exit code because Intune reads the script's output, which must match the condition set in the application requirements rule.

Getting Started

In this example, we will specify that the application can only be put on devices made by ACME (the company we built specifically for this case).

To set up and run the required script, do these things: Creating our script is the first thing we need to do. Create a new PowerShell script using the following code in the editor of your choice:

- *$Manufacturer = Get-WmiObject -Class Win32_ComputerSystem | Select-Object - ExpandProperty Manufacturer $Manufacturer*

This is just getting the name of the maker from the machine's WMI and sending it back. This needs to be added to an app now. Go to **Apps**, click on **Windows**, and then look for the app in question. Click on it and then click on "**Properties**."

- Now, click on **Edit** next to **Requirements**.
- At the bottom, click **+ Add**.
- Find the "**Requirement type**" drop-down menu and choose "**Script**."
- The **Name field** will be filled in automatically when you pick the script we just made, but you can change it if necessary.
- You can choose between 32-bit and 64-bit, user and system context, and whether the script needs to be signed.

We need to tell it what data to look for now.

There are several choices here, and you need to pick the right one. If you don't, your requirements script will fail, even if the device meets them:

If you're not sure which one you need, type the variable followed by in your script
.gettype().
This would look like this in our case:
$manufacturer.GetType()
This will give you information about the result and the name you want, which in this case is String:

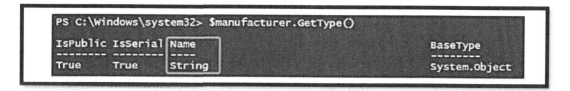

Run this code to see if it finds a number value:
- *$test = 1*

- *$Test.gettype()*

The answer will be an integer number:

- From the dropdown menu, select the right data type.
- Set your operator, which for a string is either Equals or Not Equal to. You can do more with the other types of info.
- This is going to be set to **Equals** because we only want one answer.
- Last, we need to set the value we want, which in this case is **ACME**:

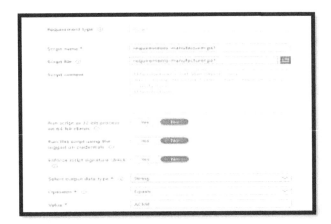

- Click **OK**.
- Click **Review + Save** on the Requirements page again.
- Make sure everything looks good, then click "**Save**."

That's all there is to do to add a custom requirements script. Let's look at some cases from real life.

Examples of custom requirements scripts

These examples will show use cases for custom requirements scripts in application deployment: This script will detect and return the manufacturer:

- *$Manufacturer = Get-WmiObject -Class Win32_ComputerSystem | Select-Object - ExpandProperty Manufacturer $Manufacturer*

This script will check whether an application is installed:

```
$File = "C:\windows\system32\notepad.exe"
if (Test-Path $File) {
write-output "Notepad detected"
}
else {
write-output "Notepad Not Detected"
}
```

In the GUI, you would be looking for a data type of String with an operator of Equals and a value of Notepad detected within the requirements configuration.

This script will look for a particular hotfix on a device:

```
$hotfixid = "KB5030219"
$hotfix = Get-HotFix | where-object HotFixID -
eq $hotfixid
if ($hotfix) {
write-output "Hotfix detected"
}
else {
write-output "Hotfix Not Detected"
}
```

For this one, we need the Hotfix detected string.

CHAPTER 12
TENANT MANAGEMENT

The options in Tenant Administration are open to all tenants and cover a wide range of topics, from the user experience to tasks that you as an administrator need to do. Being an Intune supervisor, you should know all of your options so that you can provide great service to your users and get your daily jobs done as quickly as possible.

Evaluating Your Connectors

To begin, we will talk about something important that you need to keep an eye on: third-party connections like the Apple VPP connector and Apple iOS Device Management. There is a lot to choose from, but not all of them will be useful in every situation, so keep an eye on the ones that matter to you. We will learn about the different kinds of connections here. Go to Tenant Management in the Intune site and then click on Connectors and Tokens.

This will lead you to a new section with lots of options. Now let's look at what's out there:

- **Windows enterprise certificate**: This is where you upload your code-signing certificate to your tenant if you are using it with MSIX packages. There is an important date on this page that tells you when the certificate will expire after you add it.
- **Microsoft Endpoint Configuration Manager**: If you are using Co-Management with Configuration Manager, this is where you can see the status of the Intune connection and the date and time of its last good sync.
- **Windows 365 partner connectors**: This lets estates that use Windows 365 with either Citrix or VMWare adds the connection and then check on its progress. You will need a Windows 365 license to see this screen.
- **Windows data**: Two settings can be found here for Windows files. The first is to make it possible to send diagnostic info, which is needed for Autopatch and other things. A license proof is the other choice. If you set this to "Yes," Intune will know that you have an Enterprise, Education, or AVD license (E3, E5, F3, F5). This will let you use tools that are only available for that SKU, like Remediations.
- **Apple VPP Tokens**: This is an important one if you are in charge of Apple devices because it's where you add your VPP tokens to buy and handle apps and also where you can see when they expire and renew them. This is also where you will find the sync button if you need to quickly add a paid program to Intune.
- **Managed Google Play**: This is where you can check on the Managed Google Play Connector's status and, if you want, add a scope tag to any new apps that have been added for role-based assignments.
- **Chrome Enterprise**: For setting and tracking your ChromeOS devices that have been synced from your Chrome Enterprise domain.

- **Firmware over-the-air update**: At the time this was written, this choice only worked with Zebra devices and let you set up a link between Intune and Zebra Lifeguard.
- **Microsoft Defender for Endpoint**: This is where you can check on your MDE connector's status and set cross-platform settings for the whole tenant. Don't forget that MDE needs the right licenses.
- **Mobile Threat Defense**: The Mobile Threat Defense choice lets you join third-party protection programs and see how they're doing. It's also needed for Windows MAM.
- **Partner device management (JAMF):** When you want to use JAMF compliance with Conditional access and JAMF to control your macOS devices, you can set up a connection between the two using this option.
- **Partner compliance management**: This is like JAMF, but it works with more platforms, like MobileIron, VMware, and Blackberry. It also has options that work across systems, like Android, iOS, and macOS.
- **TeamViewer connector**: If you use TeamViewer for online help, setting the connector here will make it work with Intune.
- **ServiceNow connector**: You need a license for Remote Help or Intune Suite to use this one. Configuring the connection brings information about ServiceNow issues straight to the Intune user's **Troubleshooting** and **Support** pane.
- **Certificate connectors**: This is where you can add your SCEP and NDES certificates for authentication by device.
- **Derived Credentials**: This choice is for setting certificates so that they can be used with Smart Card authentication on all systems.

Incorporating Filters

Filters are a great (and faster) way to use the assignment for All users or All devices, but only for certain people. It is also the only way to add device filters to user assignments at the time this was written. As of this writing, filters only work for Android and iOS devices and apps. To make searches based on users, you need to use a Dynamic Entra Group. You must create filters to use them in the assignment. In this section, we will discuss this.

You can choose from the following filter options:

Managed apps

- App version
- Device management type – unmanaged, Apple Business
- Manager, Kiosk, Android Enterprise, and so on
- Device manufacturer
- Device model
- Operating system version

Managed devices

- Device name
- Manufacturer
- Model
- Device category
- Operating system version
- Is rooted (iOS, Android)
- Device ownership – personal or corporate
- Enrollment profile name
- Device trust type (Windows) – hybrid or cloud-only
- Operating system SKU (Windows)

We can now create our filters that we know what they are for and what options are available.

To create your first filter, follow these steps:

- Go to **Tenant Administration** and click on **filters**. Then click **Create** and pick either **Managed devices or Managed apps**. We will be using a device filter in this case.
- Fill in the **Name** and **Description** fields, pick the **Platform** characteristic that the filter will work on, and click **Next**.
- Use the rule builder on the **Rules screen** to add the searches your rule needs. To get only devices made by ACME in this case, set **Property** to **manufacturer**, **Operator** to **Equals**, and **Value** to **ACME**. You can also change the rule manually by hitting the Edit button next to Rule syntax:

You can click Preview to see which devices will be found by the rule after you have set it. Before using the filter during assignment, this is a good way to make sure you have it set up properly. Click Next when you agree with the rule. We will discuss Scope tags later, so click **Next** for now. Last, make sure everything looks good, and then click **Create**.

Setting up Intune Roles

We set up our environment using the Intune Administrator role, but you might want to give different managers in the property different roles so that they only have the permissions they need to do their job. You can either use the built-in roles for this or create a unique role with the rights you want for it. We will go over how to set up a special job in both the GUI and PowerShell here.

- Go to Tenant Administration and then click on Roles.

NOTE: You can see what permissions you already have in the tenant by clicking on "My permissions" before you create a role. Go back to "**All roles**" and click on any of the built-in roles. This will take you to the page for that job. If you click Properties, you can see the rights that the person has been given. After that, clicking **Assignments** will let you give them to managers.

- Click **All roles**, then **+ Create**, and then choose **Intune role** to create a custom role.
- Type in the name and description of your role, and then click **Next**. We are making a basic-level role that can sync and restart a machine, as well as change the BitLocker keys and the LAPS password.
- On the Permissions page, choose the permissions that the job you're making needs, and then click **Next**.
- In this case, the options we need are **Sync devices, Rotate BitLockerKeys, Reboot now, and Rotate Local Admin Password.** They can be found under **Remote tasks**. If you're not sure what certain permission means, click on the "i" sign to find out.

NOTE: This is one time when you might want to use Scope tags to give certain permissions to only certain devices. For example, you might only want the administrator of one office to be able to run tasks on the computers in that office and not on all the computers in the tenant. The next recipe will talk about scope tags.

- In this case, we're creating this tenant-wide. After setting up, click **Next**.
- Last, make sure that all of the settings are right, then click **Create**.
- We need to give our role now that we have made it. Click on **Assignments** after clicking on the newly made role.
- Click **+ Assign**.
- Type in the **name** and **description** of your assignment, then click "**Next**."
- Now, pick an **Entra** group that this role should go with. After that, everyone in the group will get the role. When you're done, click **Next**.
- On the Scope Groups screen, you can tell these admins to only handle a certain group of users. You can choose "All Devices/All Users" to give them access everywhere, or you can name a group of devices or users that you want to give access to. The admins will only be able to do jobs against people in the chosen group if that group is chosen. After you're done, click **Next**.
- Let's look at **Scope tags** next. Since this strategy is only interested in acts that happen on devices, scope tags are not as important as scope groups. You might want to lock down special roles that let people see or change policies, though, so that different admins can only change their own set of policies. In this case, this is where you would give the scope tag that is used to make the policy.
- Once everything is set up, click **Next**. As always, make sure everything looks good and click **Create**.

Making Use of Scope Tags

To begin, we will talk about how scope groups and scope tags are different.

- Scope groups are set up inside an Intune role and tell an administrator which users or devices they can take action on for roles that have actions set up. They're like the administration units in Entra ID, where managers can be kept from seeing all of the tenant's devices and users.
- Scope tags are set up on individual things in the tenant and can be used to decide who can see these items and how. As an example, you could set up a part of your policies with a certain scope tag so that only certain managers can change it. Giving the local managers some freedom, but only on their own devices and policies, can be helpful for bigger companies with more than one management team. If you look at iOS apps, the scope tag will automatically come from the VPP token.

You need scope tags as part of your **role-based access control (RBAC)** strategy of least privileged access when you have a lot of computers spread out in different places. They work great with group tags in particular. During Autopilot enrollment, you can add group tags to your machines. Then, you can use that group tag to create an Entra group and give it to the scope tag. We can create our first scope tag now that we know how they work and what they're for.

To set up a new scope tag, do these things:

- Click on **Roles** under **Tenant Administration**.
- Click **Scope tags** and then click **+ Create** in the menu on the left.
- Type in the **Name** and **Description** of your scope tag, then click **Next**.
- Now, all you have to do is pick the groups that you want this tag to go with. We are using a static group with devices from a faraway office in this case. After setting up, click **Next**.
- Make sure your scope tag is set up properly, then click "**Create**."

Tailoring the End User Experience

- Click on **Customization** under **Tenant Administration**.

Here, we can change the default settings or, at the very bottom of the page, set up multiple policies with group assignments in case different groups of users have different needs. This could be useful for a single tenant that runs multiple sub-companies. In this case, we only want to change the usual settings, so click **Edit** next to **Settings**. **We will go through these settings section by section because there are a lot of them:**

- **Branding**: This is pretty easy. Just add your logos for dark and light backgrounds, choose colors and company names, and choose whether to show just the logo or the logo and its name.

- **Support information**: This is the details that show up in the helpline of the Company Portal. In the "Additional information" field, you can list the hours that help is available, how to be reached after hours, or a real place if you accept drop-ins.
- **Configuration**: This is where you can tell Company Portal what it can and can't do:
- **Device enrollment**: Choose whether to let the "Enroll" button work on its own.
- **Privacy Statement URL**: A link to your statement that everyone can see.
- **Privacy message**: Change the privacy warning if you want to. This is where you can do that for iOS and iPadOS.
- **Device categories**: If you have set up categories, you can stop users from choosing a group on their own.
- **App sources**: Additional apps to show on the Company Portal can be found in app sources. There are a lot of apps that you can add to your Office site, any Enterprise apps that are listed in Entra, and any Configuration Manager apps that are co-managed. Be careful with the first two options because they can quickly make Company Portal look crowded.
- **Hide features**: Select the options you don't want your users to see and click "Hide." You can hide the Remove and Reset buttons on Windows and iOS/iPadOS devices so users can't unenroll their devices. This will lead to more complaints because users will click buttons without thinking about what they're doing.

Once your settings are set up the way you want them, click Review + Save. Make sure everything looks good, then click "Save."

Distributing Organizational Messages

Organizational messages are a way to show important information on end-user devices that only work with Windows.

This kind of message can show up in three places:

- **Taskbar messages**: this show up just above the toolbar and look like regular toast notifications.
- **Notification area messages**: These show up in the notification area, and they work with email alerts, Teams messages, and other things.
- **Get Started app messages**: The messages in the Get Started app only need to be run once after licensing. They show up in the Get Started app.

You must make sure you have the right license to use group messages before you go any further. You will need one of these licenses:

- Microsoft 365 E3
- Microsoft 365 E5
- Windows 10/11 Enterprise E3 with Intune Plan 1
- Windows 10/11 Enterprise E5 with Intune Plan 1

For these options, you can send different kinds of messages. We can set up a group message now that we understand what it is.

How to do it...

- Click on **Tenant Administration** and then **organizational messages**. Click **Message** at the top and then click **+ Create**.
- Choose your Message type and theme in the pop-up window, and then click OK. With an Important move, we will create a Taskbar message in this case.

There is no message itself, so we need to add a link to it on the web. It could be a link to a private page or some kind of news story.

- Choose the language you want to use and give your message a name. You can also add a logo and a link. Then click Next: Schedule.

Please note that you would need to include two texts in the "Get Started" app message.

- You can set a time for your campaign to run and how often you want the message to show up here. The only choice you have when you use **Get Started** is **Repeat frequency,** which tells you how long the message will be shown, but it also has the **Always On** option. After setting up, click **Next**: **Scope tags**.
- Add Scope tags here if you need to give rights to other people; otherwise, click Next: Assignments.
- Be sure to set up the **Assignments page** correctly because it's only where you can give to users or user-based groups. It will only target the users within a mixed group. If it's a message for the whole company, you can also choose to send it to all users.
- Once everything is set up, click **Next: Review + Create.**

Deploying custom notifications

As was already said, organizational messages only work on Windows devices. You can send custom alerts to Android and iOS devices. These will show up in the device's alerts area. These may show up on a lock screen depending on how your security is set up, so please check your settings again before using this way to send any private information.

To set up and send a custom message, just follow these easy steps:

- Go to Tenant Administration and click on Custom Notifications.
- Give your message a Title and Content, and then click Next.
- Assign tasks as needed. Once more, it's only for users; you can't choose "All Users" here. When you're done, click Next.
- Finally, check to make sure everything is right, and then click Create.

Establishing Terms and Conditions

Users should accept organizational rules when enrolling a device, especially if they are doing so from home or using Bring Your Device (BYOD). Terms and Conditions in Intune and Terms of Use within Entra Conditional Access are the two options available for doing this. Terms of use are significantly more powerful and give you more freedom, but we will cover both options here to give you a full picture. Let's learn how to set up our options now that we've seen them. To begin, we will look at Intune's terms and conditions, which are a very simple list of rules that the user must agree to.

Setting up terms and conditions

- Go to Tenant Administration first, then Terms and Conditions. Press the + Create.
- Type in the name and description of your policy, and then click **Next**.
- Now, enter the policy's Title, Summary of Terms, and real Terms and Conditions. These are just plain text; we need the terms and conditions in Entra for pictures, links, and other things.
- After going through the steps, click Next.
- Add your Scope tags if you need to give other people access. In that case, just click Next.
- Let's look at the assignment for this term. So that you can catch as much as possible, you should stick to user assignments here. You can also give to All Users if you need to. Click Next.
- Finally, check to make sure everything is right, and then click **Create**.

That's all there is to do for the Intune terms and conditions. Let us now look at those that Entra has to give.

Configuring Entra's Terms of Use

We can get to these Entra settings through the Intune site, even though they are Entra settings. To get to Conditional Access, go to Endpoint Security.

- Click on Terms of Use under Manage in the menu and click + New Terms.
- Choose a Name, a Title, and a Language, and then add your PDF.
- **Here, we have a few options:**
  - **Require users to expand the terms of use**: The Terms of Use must be read by all users.
  - **Require users to consent on every device**: Users can agree to everything at once, or you can ask them each time they use a device.
  - **Expire consents**: "Expire consents" means that these rules must be followed right away, and any earlier consent must be thrown out.
  - **Duration before re-acceptance required (days):** How long before a user needs to re-accept
- Finally, you can choose Create conditional access policy later, where you can add to an existing policy in the Grant access section, or you can choose Create new policy to execute these rules. We will use a strategy that is already in place in this case:

- Right now, click "**Create**." You will be taken to the well-known **Conditional Access Policy screen** if you selected to create a new policy, where you can customize it as needed.

Configuring Multi-Admin Approvals

- Go to Tenant Administration and click on Multi-Admin Approval.

You can see all the requests that are still being processed (All requests), all the requests that you have sent (My requests), and the policies that have been set up (Access policies).

- **Access Policies** should be selected, then click **+ Create**.
- Choose the **name** and **description** of your policy, as well as whether it applies to Script or App. After that, click **Next**.
- Choose an Approvers group on the screen that shows up. This group should have administrators who can accept requests. After you're done, click Next.
- Last, make sure everything looks good, and then click Create.
- We will now look at how to use them. You will be asked to give a business reason when you add a new program or script. We don't have a "Create" button; instead, we have a "Submit for approval" button.
- This is where we can see the request in Multi-Admin Approval.

- If you log in as an approver and click on **"Business justification,"** a flyout will appear with information about the request, such as what was written in the script and why it was sent in.
- Type some notes at the bottom of the flyout, and then click either "**Approve request**" or **"Reject request."**
- The person who made the request must then complete it in the **Multi-Admin Approval site.** This will add the application or script and make it ready to be given. You can get information from the data in the request when you hit the Create button. This information is then sent back to Graph.

Verifying Your Tenant Version

- Go to Tenant Administration and click on Tenant status.

- In the first tab, you can see information about your tenant, such as the version and position of the tenant:

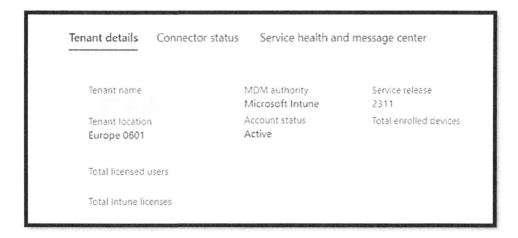

- The list of set connections will be shown quickly on the Connector status tab. In this case, if you notice any problems, you can use the earlier method to find out more (Reviewing your connections).
- Finally, the **Service health and message center** area will show you any major problems with Microsoft, any events happening in your tenant that you need to handle, and any messages. Messages usually have to do with new features, changes, or other things.

Utilizing Intune's Troubleshooting Tools

- Go to **Troubleshooting** and click on **Support**. Then, from the menu, click **Troubleshoot**.
- Select a person from the list and all of their information will be taken care of immediately.
- The first thing we need to do is check the User status to make sure there aren't any simple problems, like a user who isn't authorized or is blocked.
- The **Summary** screen shows a summary of all the information for the user, including devices, policies, compliance, apps, and more.
- **You can use the following tabs:**
  o **Devices**: All of the user's devices, including Intune compliance, Entra compliance, and the state of failed app install.
  o **Groups**: "Groups" are the Entra groups that the person is a part of.
  o **Policy**: The policies that have been given to the person.
  o **Applications**: The cross-platform apps that the user has been given access to, along with the number of devices that can run them.
  o **App protection policy**: These are the app security policies that have been given to the user and their current status.
  o **Updates**: The update policies that have been put on the user's devices.

- **Enrollment restrictions**: The platform's limitations and restrictions that apply to this person are listed under Enrollment Restrictions. This will tell us if the person has reached their limit and can't enroll any more devices by comparing it to the Devices tab.
- **Diagnostics**: The results of any tests that were asked for.

To ask for diagnostics, go to the device in question and press the button that says "**Collect Diagnostics.**" After some time, a ZIP file with all of the machine's important data will be sent out.

Setting up Enrollment Notifications

To set up registration alerts for your users, do these steps:

- To begin, go to **Devices** and then click on **Enrollment**. Select the tab for the site where you want to set up the alerts. Each site will need its policy.
- Select **Enrollment Notifications** and then click on **+ Create notification**.
- Type in the name and description of your notice, then click **Next**.
- You can choose what kind of message to send on the **Notification Settings** screen. You can send a **Push notification**, an **Email notification**, or both.
- For a **push notification**, all you need is the following in the title and text:

- You can choose from more options for an **email notification:**
  - You can change the email's **Subject** and **Message**, and if you turn on the raw HTML editor, you can add HTML.
  - You can add a heading.
- You can also put the name of the company, how to reach you, and a link to the company Portal, where users can see the devices they have enrolled. All of this information comes from the **Tenant Administration** modification settings. One very helpful feature is the ability to add information about the device to the bottom. This way, the user can see

which device was enrolled and see if any questions give the information when reporting it.

- After setting up, click **Next**.
- Add a Scope tag value if you want to give someone else access to the notifications. Click **Next** if not.
- Since the device won't be available until after registration, **assignment** must be done at the user level. So, either choose a group of users or send to everyone. After that, click **Next**.
- Finally, check to make sure everything is right, and then click **Create**.

Configuring Device Restrictions

This page has two settings that you can change: device limit restrictions and device platform restrictions. First, we will look at limits on devices.

Device limit restrictions

To limit the number of devices you can use, do these things:

- Go to **Devices** and click on **Enrollment**.
- Select a platform and click on **Device limit restriction.**

You can change the default restriction, which affects everyone, or create new restrictions here. The queries for the restrictions are run in numerical order, with the largest number being run first. It stops looking at other policies as soon as it finds the one that applies to the person. Create extra policies if you need to set different restrictions for different groups of users. But if you want a general method, all you have to do is change the usual policy. We are going to add a new policy to this case to give more control.

- Press **+ Create restriction**.
- Give the policy a **name** and a **description**.
- Click on **Device Limit** and pick a limit. This can be anywhere from 1 to 15 devices.

NOTE: Remember the rules for cleaning up your device here. If the device limit is set to 1, and a person gets a new computer, you will have to remove the old one manually before they can add the new one. It shouldn't be dangerous to have this number higher if you have personal devices turned off since the devices will all belong to the company anyway.

- Once everything is set up, click **Next**.
- Add a Scope tag value here if you want to give this policy to someone. Click **Next** if not.
- Give the policy the right assignment on the **Assignments** screen. Since that is the default assignment, you can't choose "All Users." Instead, you will need to choose a user group here. When you're done, click **Next**.

- The last step is to make sure that your restriction limit and assignment look good, and then click **Create**.

This completes setting the device's restrictions. Let's look at the restrictions on device platforms now.

Device platform restrictions

What we can and can't do on our medium is more specific. You can either change the default policy, which is used by all platforms, or you can create custom policies for each one. In this case, we are going to change the usual strategy because we want to stop BYOD registration across all platforms.

To set up device platform restrictions, do the following:

- Go to **Devices** and click on **Enrollment**.
- Select a platform and click on **Device platform restriction.**
- Now, click on the blue text that says "**All Users.**"
- You need to go to **Properties** and click on the **Edit** text next to **Platform settings**.

You can choose which platforms; operating system versions, personal devices, and makers (only for Android) you want to fully accept. If you choose to block based on version, make sure you keep checking the settings as new versions come out and older ones are no longer supported. If you don't, you might end up stopping new devices or letting everything through.

As support for Android Device Administrator is coming to an end, we are going to stop that as well as all personally owned devices:

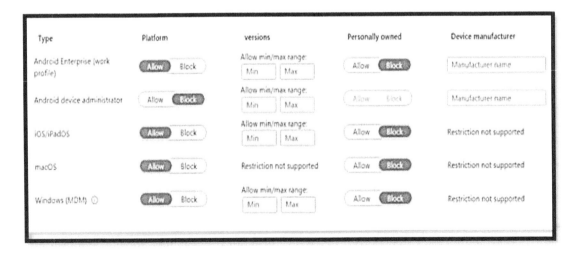

Type	Platform	versions	Personally owned	Device manufacturer
Android Enterprise (work profile)	Allow / Block	Allow min/max range: Min / Max	Allow / Block	Manufacturer name
Android device administrator	Allow / Block	Allow min/max range: Min / Max	Allow / Block	Manufacturer name
iOS/iPadOS	Allow / Block	Allow min/max range: Min / Max	Allow / Block	Restriction not supported
macOS	Allow / Block	Restriction not supported	Allow / Block	Restriction not supported
Windows (MDM)	Allow / Block	Allow min/max range: Min / Max	Allow / Block	Restriction not supported

- Once everything is set up, click **Review + Save.**

These rules are already set at the tenant level, so there are no assignment or scope tags here. Create individual policies to put on top of the baseline if you need different settings for different groups or want to give access to others.

- Finally, make sure everything looks good, then click "**Save**."

Establishing Quiet Time Policies

- Go to **Apps** and then **Quiet Time** to set up Quiet Time policies.
- Click on the **Policies** tab and then click on **+ Create Policy**.
- From the drop-down menu, choose the **Policy type** number you want to change, then click **Create**.
- Enter the **name** and **description** of your policy, and then click "**Next**."
- Giving the person the power to change the settings is the first thing you can do here. Should you not have any strict needs, leave this set to Yes.
- You can set alerts to be quiet at certain times of the day in the **Certain Hours** section. Set these times around the times you expect your staff to work. Keep in mind that they can change these at any time. Remove the check marks from Saturday and Sunday in this section if you want to stop alerts on the weekends.
- Pick out your days off, like Saturday and Sunday, in the "**Allday**" section. If you set it to "**Require**" and "**Configured**," it should choose those days for you automatically.
- After setting up, click **Next**.
- Add a **Scope tag value** if you want to give someone else access. Click **Next** if not.
- Consider the company as a whole when considering your Assignments. If you have people who work on call, like IT staff, makes sure they are not covered by the policy. Also, some executives may work longer hours and don't want to have to change the settings manually all the time, so it might be best to leave them out.

Consider making multiple policies to reflect the different shift times if you have them. However, you would probably need to integrate your HR system to keep track of which users are in which groups based on their shift schedules.

- Click **Next** when you're done setting up your assignments.
- Finally, check to make sure everything is right, and then click **Create**.

The basic settings are all the same when creating a Date Range policy, but the Configuration settings only allow you to choose a date range.

CHAPTER 13

GETTING STARTED WITH INTUNE SUITE

How to Deploy and Utilize Remote Help

You can get remote assistance for Windows, macOS, and Android with remote help. It lets you connect devices that aren't signed up and can be fully controlled with custom Intune roles and flexible role-based access control (RBAC). To use Remote Help, you need more than one thing. Configuring the policies and RBAC will be talked about in this section. However, you need to have already deployed the apps on your devices. **We will now go over setting an RBAC role to allow certain admins to use Remote Help and allow it in the property.**

- Go to **Tenant Administration** and click on **Remote Help** to turn on Remote Help.
- Go to **Settings** and click on **Configure**.
- In the drop-down menu, change **Enable Remote Help** to **Enabled**. You can also allow or block chat here, as well as turn on Remote Help for unenrolled devices.
- Click **Save** when everything is set up the way you want it.
- We can now set up our new role:
  - ○ **Tenant administration**s followed by roles are the next things you should click.
  - ○ Go to **Create** and pick the **Intune role.**
- Type in your **name** and a **description**, then click "**Next.**"
- Scroll down to the Remote Help app in the role list and choose your access for that role. You can pick one of these:
  - ○ **View screen**: Simple view-only access
  - ○ **Elevation**: Allows the admin to UAC elevate on the machine
  - ○ **Unattended control**: The end user doesn't have to permit for this to work.
  - ○ **Take full control**: This option lets the administrator run the computer instead of just viewing it.

For various admin levels, you might want to create various roles.

- Once everything is set up, click **Next**.
- On the next screen, you can add your scope tags if you want to put the roles on a certain business unit. When you're done, click **Next**.
- Last, make sure everything looks good, and then click **Create**.

Exploring Microsoft Tunnel for Mobile Application Management

MAM is a way to make apps link to a VPN server on a device that is not controlled and runs Android or iOS. The Microsoft Tunnel for MAM adds to the features of the Tunnel VPN. Because of this, the Microsoft Tunnel access to your on-premises system must be live and linked.

171

To set up Microsoft Tunnel for your mobile apps, do the following:

- Go to **Apps** and pick **App protection policies.**
- Create a new policy or make changes to an existing one.
- Scroll to the bottom of the **Data Protection** screen and set **Start Microsoft Tunnel connection on app-launch** to **True**.
- Depending on whether you were editing an existing policy or creating a new one, click **Save** or **create** to save your changes.

This is the last step in setting up Microsoft Tunnel for MAM.

Assessing Device Anomalies

Another part of Intune Suite is Advanced Endpoint Analytics, which is made up of three parts:

- **Device anomaly detection**: This feature uses machine learning to look for patterns across your estate and let you know about any possible problems.
- **Custom device scopes**: This lets you let different groups of managers have different rights by adding scope tags to the Endpoint Analytics Reports. As an example, you could let a business team look at reports for only the devices they own.
- **Enhanced device timeline**: This makes the past of events for each device longer so you can see more of what's been going on.

Then, you can use Azure Automation's anomaly detection to send email or Teams alerts automatically when problems are found. Now that we know what the parts are, we can learn how to look at our device's strange behavior.

- To begin, go to **Reports** and click on **Endpoint statistics.**
- On the main screen, click on **Anomalies** at the very top.
- This is where you can see all the strange things that your devices have found. It is set to sort them by intensity by default, but you can change it to any column.
- Clicking on a title will show more information, such as the devices that are affected and any links (device association groups) between those devices and the problem that was found.

When it comes to proactive device support, device anomaly detection is a great tool. It can also give any problems that need to be reported to a hardware seller extra weight.

Setting Up Endpoint Privilege Management

Endpoint Privilege Management (EPM) lets you give end users more access to certain apps without giving them full control over the device. For example, this could be for a business app that needs to be elevated or for your staff to be able to use certain tools on devices. We can set up rules for EPM so that it can either automatically elevate or need to be approved first.

How to do it...

To begin, we will go over how to set up EPM in the UI:

- In **Endpoint Security**, find **Endpoint Privilege Management** and click on it.
- To begin, we need to make a settings policy. To do this, click **Create** and then choose **Windows 10 and later** and **Elevation settings policy**. Then press the "**Create**" button.
- Give your policy a **name** and a **description**, then click **Next**.
- The first thing we need to do on this screen is turn on EPM. Then we can choose which diagnostics data to report on: (**Diagnostic data only, diagnostic data and all endpoint elevations,** or **Diagnostic data and managed endpoint elevations only**). You can also set a **Default elevation response** (**Not configured, Deny all requests,** or **require user confirmation**).
- Once everything is set up the way you want it, click **Next**:

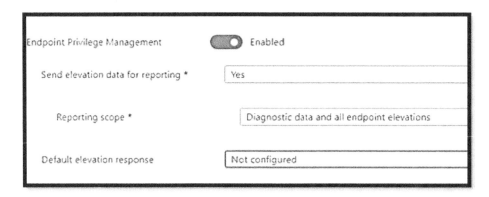

- Add your scope tags on the next screen if you need to give rights to a certain group of managers. If not, just click **Next**.
- Give the policy as required. This is a setting that affects the whole lease if you're not using scope tags. It makes sense to apply it to **All users or All devices**. When you're done, click **Next**.
- Last, make sure everything looks good, and then click **Create**.
- Since EPM is now set up at the tenant level, we can add our first rule to let an application level up:
- Click **Create Policy** under **Endpoint security** > **Endpoint Privilege Management** menu blade. In the pop-up menu that appears, choose Windows 10 and later, and then click Elevation rules policy. After that, click **Create**.
- Choose a **name** and a **description** for your coverage. A good name practice will be helpful here because you might end up with multiple policies for your various EPM rules. After that, click **Next**.
- When you click the "**Add**" button on the "**Configuration settings**" screen, you can add more than one app. You will see that there is already something there, so click **+ Edit instance** to change this one:

- In the fly-out, give the Rule a **name** and a **description**.
- In **Elevation conditions**, you can choose whether this app will accept itself or if the user needs to confirm with credentials (**Windows authentication**) or a chosen reason (**Business justification**). These are good for reviewing, so it's worth considering.
- You can also choose what to do with child tasks. You can either make them instantly accept or refuse, or you can make them need their own rule. You can choose in what context Notepad will be opened if, say, you raise the **Command Prompt** application and the user tries to open it.
- We will now talk about the file information, which is what **Intune and Windows** use to decide if the app can be raised. For setting the program here, you have two options.

For **filehash**, which you can get by running this PowerShell script, you can use

- *Get-filehash -path "path to executable"*

You can also send a certificate that the file can use instead.

The following PowerShell function can be used to export a certificate:

- *Get-AuthenticodeSignature -FilePath "path to executable"*

Using the Reusable Settings option, you can use the same license for more than one app from the same developer. Also, you need to enter a File name value here. You can also add the numbers for File path, Minimum version, File description, Product name, and Internal name if you want to.

- Once everything is set up, click **Save** and then **Next**.
- If you need to assign, do it here on the Scope tags screen, then click **Next**.
- Assign tasks as needed. Follow the least privilege model here, which means that assignments should be kept to a minimum, especially if child processes are allowed. After setting up, click Next.
- Last, make sure everything looks good, and then click **Create**.

CHAPTER 14
LOOKING AT REPORTING TECHNICAL REQUIREMENTS

We will now keep looking at the ready-made reports that are out there. We will also show you how to export the data so that you can use it in Power BI and Azure, as well as the more advanced Windows Update reporting that you can do with Log Analytics. Reporting is a key part of any Intune setting for getting a point-in-time (PIT) picture of where you stand, especially if the organization's leaders ask for it. This part will show you the reports that come with Intune and how to run them manually or automatically.

How to Examine Device Management Reports

Click the Reports button in the menu to get to the device management reports. All of these can be found in Device settings. Now that we have the reports, we can look at each one by one. We will go over the many available reports and the information that is in them here.

Reviewing device compliance

The following steps will be used to check device compliance:

If you want to see reports on device compliance, go to Device Compliance and click on the Reports tab at the top. To begin, we will go over what each of the following reports can do, and then we will talk about how to run them. The guidelines for running the reports will apply to all of them, except for device compliance trends.

- **Device compliance**: This shows a list of all the devices and what state of compliance they are in. Everyone in charge will be interested in this study because it is useful. You can export it, but you can't click on it to see which devices are not compliant. Some good filtering and search tools are built in.
- **Device compliance trends**: This is an easy image that shows how device compliance has changed over the last 60 days. There is only the filtering choice. There is no exit or click-through.
- **Noncompliant devices and settings**: These are the noncompliant devices and settings report. It goes into more detail than the Device compliance report you just saw and is usually the most useful. It shows the name of the device and then the specific setting(s) in the compliance policy(s) that are causing the non-compliance. This can look at each setting in your custom policy if you have one. Additionally, it reports whether there is a mistake or if the setting is just not right. It can sort based on titles and has filtering and searching tools.

- **Devices without compliance policy**: This report is pretty simple; it just shows all the devices that don't have any compliance policies given to them. This should be empty, so it is always worth checking, especially if you have setup devices that aren't listed as compliant (it will tell you what they are set to and how to change them). You can sort and find by device name, as well as filter by OS and who owns the device. This should be more than enough for a simple report.
- **Setting compliance**: This report shows all the compliance settings for all policies and platforms, along with the numbers for meeting and not meeting compliance for each setting. Along with finding and filtering, you can choose to sort all fields, and you can click through to see which devices are compliant or not compliant for each setting. This report can help you find patterns in the whole estate, especially if you find a lot of devices that don't follow the rules and want to see if there are any patterns.
- **Policy compliance**: This report is similar to the last one, but instead of looking at individual settings, it looks at the policy level and shows device compliance and non-compliance per policy. Again, you can use this to determine which policy is causing a lot of devices to be blocked for not following the rules all of a sudden. For farms with a lot of policies, this feature helps you quickly find the report where a certain setting is located. You can search, filter, and sort by column, just like the other ones.

To run these reports, except for Device compliance trends, all you have to do is click the **Generate report** (or **Generate** again) button. The site will let you know when the report is ready, but it can take a few minutes to finish. To run the **Device compliance trends** report, all you have to do is click the "**Refresh**" button. Our device compliance reports have been examined and made.

Checking device configuration

We can now look at the device setup report to see how the policies are going:

- To get to this report, click Reports, then Device Configuration, and finally the Reports tab at the top. Then, click on Profile configuration status.
- Press Generate report, or press Generate again if you have already run the report.
- This message will be sent to you once it's been generated:

- This report shows a list of all profiles across all operating systems. - It also counts the number of times each profile has been marked as **Success**, **Error**, or **Conflict**.

Besides being able to export, you can also look for a profile by name or sort by any title. You can also filter by OS and profile type. Sorting is a great way to find patterns in policies that don't agree with each other or policies that have errors. People with a lot of success are less of a worry.

TIP: You can't click on any of the rows in this report, so you can't drill down. You can only view it. That's all there is to device configuration. At this point, we can look at Group Policy analytics.

Reviewing Group Policy analytics

This report is used with Group policy analytics. It just shows the results of all the loaded group policies and the current state of the settings in them. When the Summary screen first comes up, it will show a list of the settings that were found and whether they are ready to be imported into Intune.

Create your report by following these guidelines:

- Go to **Reports** and then **Group Policy Analytics** to get to it. After getting there, click on **Reports** and then on **Group Policy Migration Readiness**.
- If you have already done this, click **Generate** or **Generate again** once you are in the report.
- Once the report is done, there is the standard Export button, as well as a useful overview and a pretty strong filter:

You can sort by each title and look at almost anything. It's not possible to click through here, but this report tells us what can and cannot be moved. You would have to go back to the Group Policy Analytics page in Devices to do any more work. While loading a lot of settings at once is never a good idea, this report will at least show you which settings need to be looked at and either changed or set up using a different way, like policy ingestion, custom policy, or PowerShell scripting.

Setting Name ↑↓	Group Policy Setti... ↑↓	Migration Readiness ↑↓	Min OS Version ↑↓	Scope ↑↓	Profile Type ↑↓
Choose drive encryptio...	Windows Components/...	Ready for migration	15063	Computer	Device configuration: All
Choose drive encryptio...	Windows Components/...	Ready for migration	15063	Computer	Device configuration: All
Choose drive encryptio...	Windows Components/...	Ready for migration	15063	Computer	Device configuration: All
Choose drive encryptio...	Windows Components/...	Ready for migration	15063	Computer	Device configuration: All
Choose drive encryptio...	Windows Components/...	Not supported	0	Computer	Not supported
Choose drive encryptio...	Windows Components/...	Not supported	0	Computer	Not supported
Choose drive encryptio...	Windows Components/...	Not supported	0	Computer	Not supported
Choose drive encryptio...	Windows Components/...	Not supported	0	Computer	Not supported
Do not keep history of r...	Start Menu and Taskbar	Ready for migration	17755	Computer	Device configuration: All
Turn off File History	Windows Components/...	Ready for migration	18362	Computer	Device configuration: All

Now that we've looked over the Group Policy analytics reports, we can see what's out there for devices that are co-managed.

Cloud-attached devices

The Co-Management Eligibility and Co-Managed Workloads reports are only useful for places that use Configuration Manager and want to look into co-management. In the Intune site, go to **Reports | Cloud Attached Devices** and then click on the **Reports tab** to see these reports. We can now look at what's in these reports.

Co-Management Eligibility

This report tells you what's going on with cloud-connected devices and if they can be co-managed. Click **Generate report** or **Generate again** to run the report. When run, this will show basic information about the devices and whether they are eligible for each one. You can sort, filter, export, and search on the headers, just like you can on the other reports.

Co-Managed Workloads

You can choose which tasks are handled by Intune and which are handled by Configuration Manager when you configure co-management. If you run this report, it will show you a list of your devices and the tasks that are set up for each one. This is a good tool for fixing problems if you run into them. Click **Generate Report** or **Generate Again**, just like you did with the last report. For both the Co-Management Eligibility report and this one, there is a strong filter that lets you quickly look for specific settings. But you can only find and sort by device name and ID, so use the categories instead. That's all we have to say about what information is in device management reports and how to run them. Now we can look at how to make these automatic.

Analyzing Endpoint Security Reports for Insights

Next, we'll look at the very important security reports. You might have security teams or a security operations center (SOC) that need to keep an eye on these, even if you don't check them yourself. If all goes well, everything that is being watched here will be covered in a compliance policy. But in case something goes wrong, reports are always helpful. You can find all the endpoint security reports that are mentioned in this section by going to Reports and then Endpoint Security. We can go through each report once we've found the Reports menu in the UI.

Reviewing Microsoft Defender Antivirus

Go to the **Endpoint security reports** section, click on **Microsoft Defender Antivirus,** and then click on the **Reports tab**. This will take you to where our two reports are. We will talk about both of them in more depth here.

Antivirus agent status

This report tells you everything you need to know about the protection software on all of your devices. You can quickly find any tools that are at risk, figure out which part is broken, and fix the problem. Click **Generate report or Generate again** to make the report. After running the report, you should have a useful map that shows the status of your devices. It should be mostly green, if not all green. There is a good filter, a simple search tool, and the option to group by header.

NOTE: There is a lot of information to process, and there is a big scroll bar at the bottom. Make sure that everything is checked, especially if a device is reporting problems.

Detected malware

This report shows a list of all the devices that are infected or have been affected in the past. It also shows what malware was found and how many times it was found. Just like before, click **Generate report or Generate again.** Run it, and then use the filter, search, and sort by header options. There is also a useful graph that shows the overall status. This report is pretty important because it lets you keep an eye on devices that are infected or that keep breaking the rules. After looking at antivirus reports, it makes sense to look at firewall reports next.

Reviewing firewall reports

In the firewall report, you can see how Windows Firewall is working on all of your devices. The paper is easy to read and useful. To make the report, do these things:

- Click **Firewall** and then click **MDM Firewall status** for Windows 10 and later to get to this report. You will see that this report doesn't have any tabs.
- Press **"Generate report" or "Generate again."**

Once the report is generated, you will see a screen that looks like the one you saw before. It will have a map showing the general state, a strong filter, and the option to search and sort on any field. In reality, you'll only be interested in the ones where the firewall is turned off, so you can filter or sort them. Either way, the result will be the same. We have made and looked over computer security reports by following these steps. We can now think about automating them.

Assessing Endpoint Analytics Reports for Optimization

Endpoint analytics is a real gold mine of data that shows you not only data about your estate but also a comparison to other organizations of the same size. We won't tell you how to run the endpoint analytics reports because they are all display-and-export reports. Instead, we will talk about what each report does and how it can help you. To quickly and easily get the data from any of the reports, we will then create a single automatic script.

- Go to **Reports** and click on **Endpoint Analytics** to find these reports.
- Click on **Settings** and make sure that the setting for the **Intune data collection policy** says **"Connected."**

We can look at what all of our endpoint analytics reports show now that we know where to find them.

Startup performance

The starting performance, from hitting the button to having a useful screen, is examined in this collection of reports. Then, it compares this to a standard in the industry to give you an idea of how your devices and setup stack up.

You can get more information about the following things here:

- **Model performance**: all models in the tenant (at least 10 devices).

- **Device performance**: This and the model performance also show the type of drive, which is a great way to see how much performance improves with a Solid State
- This test compares **Drive/nonvolatile memory express (SSD/NVMe)** to an old hard drive that spins. This can help with business cases and also find drives that are starting to fail.
- **Startup processes**: A list of all the startup processes that have been found, along with the number of devices that have been found and how long they are taking to start up.
- **Restart frequency**: This one is very helpful because it shows how often the computer restarts and what caused them over the last 30 days. If you put out a program or driver update, this is a good place to look to see if any sudden reboots might be related to that. You might also want to check out Anomaly Detection in Advanced Endpoint Analytics.

As we've already looked at startup performance, we can now look at application reliability.

Application reliability

These reports go all the way down to the application level and look at crashes that happen in applications. On the first screen, you can see the reliability number compared to the baseline and the top 14 days of spam.

The following are in the reports:

- **App performance**: A list of all the apps that have been found, how many devices use them, how long they're used, and how many times they've crashed in the last 14 days. This report is helpful because it shows how often the app is used. This means that an app that crashes a lot but is highly used is not as dangerous as an app that crashes all the time but is rarely used.
- **Model performance**: This checks how well each application works on each model of device to see if there are patterns in crashes that could be caused by hardware problems. This is especially helpful for your more resource-intensive apps like CAD or graphics programs.
- **Device performance**: This goes even deeper into the details of the device and shows a list of program crashes for each machine, along with the device's health state. When a user comments about app crashes or device performance, you might find this one helpful. If the numbers are much worse on one device than on others, it could also mean that the hardware is broken.
- **OS version performance**: A useful report when upgrading OS. Check the performance of this after deploying to the test and pilot rings to see if there are any clear signs of performance loss before deploying to the bigger estate. In the same way, a clear boost in performance might help persuade users to update.

Work-from-anywhere reports are the next ones we'll look over.

Work from anywhere

These reports are mostly about how your devices are handled in the cloud, whether they are Autopilot builds or Intune joined (or co-managed). There is, however, one important study here that shows how ready your devices are for Windows 11 by looking at all of their hardware needs.

These are the reports:

- **Model performance:** a count of each model and the effects of managing the cloud and making Windows work with it. It's easy to see which types won't work with Windows 11 and get an idea of how many devices will need to be replaced during this process. In the Windows report, you can get exact numbers.
- **Device performance:** The same as in the last report, but for each device. It's certainly not as useful now, though, since the next reports will look at single settings.
- **Windows:** A very important report that looks at every device found and names those that can run Windows 11. It will show whether it passed or failed and also explain why it failed in case that is something that can be fixed more quickly. Make sure you scroll to the end to see the important columns.
- **Cloud identity:** It will show you the devices and the type of control they have (Microsoft Entra Joined or Microsoft Entra Hybrid Joined). It's likely not as useful as other reports.
- **Cloud management:** Intune or Configuration Manager are two examples of control tools for devices that are shown here. The compliance strategy is also shown. It can be a quick way to get data or do simple fixing in a split setting.
- **Cloud provisioning:** This shows your devices and the information about Autopilot that goes with them. It does have filtering, which may be useful, and gives a little more detail than the Device Enrollment screen.

This is the end of the Work from Anywhere reports. Now, we can examine Resource performance reports.

Resource performance

These two reports are for Windows 365 Cloud PCs. They let you see how your given devices are running and let you know if you need to get a higher license to meet the needs of the device or a lower license to save money if the devices aren't being used much.

Here are the available reports:

- **Model performance:** CPU and RAM scores for each type of device. There may need to be a license boost for the whole farm if you see that one type is having more trouble.
- **Device performance:** This examines each device's performance so that you can identify any devices that might be having trouble or aren't being used enough and re-license as needed. This is the one you should keep an eye on the most to keep your costs down since you can always scale up again if you need to. To see how well users can handle a lower

specification, it is often best to start with that. This is especially true for Windows 365, which runs on the Microsoft network and will greatly improve performance on web-based apps.

Remoting connection

This checks the performance of your Windows 365 devices when talking to the cloud PC from a host machine. It looks at the speed of the most recent connection, the average speed, and the total rate.

The following reports are in it:

- **Model performance**: This shows how long it takes for cloud PCs to go back and forth and sign in. The RTT shouldn't change much at the device level, so pay attention to the sign-in time if a particular model is greatly affecting the user experience.
- **Device performance**: This looks at each device. For example, some users may need a faster machine because they have to log in to more apps. The RTT is more useful here because it could mean that the host machine is having trouble connecting to the network.

Utilizing Intune Data Warehouse with Power BI for Enhanced Analysis

Anyone who has used Power BI before will know that it is a very powerful reporting tool. Intune adds a lot of extra features and lets you change what you can do out of the box. Power BI can be used with Intune Data Warehouse, which is great, and there are even tools that are already set up to help you get started.

How to do it...

- Click on **Data Warehouse** in the **Reports** menu.
- You can manually import data by clicking on the URL on this screen, but for this case, we will use the already-set-up template.
- For now, click on the Get Power BI app link.
- Click **Get it now** in the **Intune Compliance (Data Warehouse)** app box. This will take you to Power BI, and after a short time, it will show up in your list of apps:

- Click on the app that was just added.
- Click on Compliance Overview. Samples are being used, so don't worry.
- Click on Connect your data.
- On the Connect to Intune Compliance (Data Warehouse) screen, click Next as we do not have any parameters in this application.
- Choose the level of privacy type, then click Sign in and connect.
- Verify your identity in the pop-up window when asked (you may need to accept pop-ups).
- Your data will change to the same info after a minute.
- You can change your data as needed now that it is linked.

Monitoring Windows Updates through Reporting Tools

Windows Update reports are probably the most useful and most-used reports in Intune. This is because keeping track of the progress of Windows Updates is a key part of keeping the whole farm safe. The built-in reports will be examined first, and then Log Analytics will be introduced in the next section for even more control. The inputs can't be automated because they need a lot of extra choices to make these reports. It would take the same number of text boxes and clicks to get the same result. This section will not talk about automating them because of this. If this is interesting to you, though, it uses the same POST calls to export and import as many of the other reports.

- Click on Reports in the Intune site, then click on Windows updates, and finally click on the Reports tab.
- Since there are several reports here, we will begin by looking at how to run them and then move on to talking about what each report contains.
- Select from the accessible reports. We will use the Windows Feature Update Report in this case.

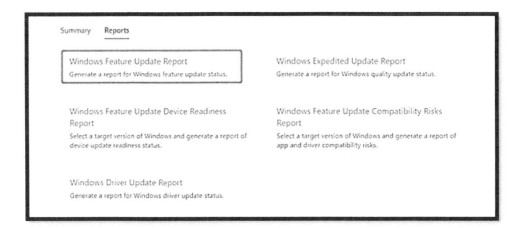

You will need to click the blue text on the right side of each report to choose what to report on. In this case, we need to click on an update ring on the right profile. Once you've made your choice, a button that says "Generate report" will appear. Click it. You will be told when the report is ready to be seen.

Now that we know how to run the reports, let's see what they show:

- **Windows Feature Update Report**: The Windows Feature Update Report will show the progress of the update for all devices in the chosen policy or ring when delivering feature updates like 22H2.
- **Windows Expedited Update Report**: This is like the last report, but it only shows Quality updates (if they are set up since they need extra licensing).
- **Windows Feature Update Device Readiness Report**: The Windows Feature Update Device Readiness Report also needs extra licensing and license checking to be turned on. Once it's turned on, you can pick an OS version, and it will let you know if your devices are ready to receive the update. When making plans for updates, this report is very helpful.
- **Windows Feature Update Compatibility Risks Report**: This is another report that is very helpful for planning updates. This one will show you a list of any programs or tools that don't work with the operating system you chose. It also needs the same licenses and other requirements as before.
- **Windows Driver Update Report:** If you are using the new driver update feature, this will show you how the chosen driver is being installed across your estate.

We can look at making this better by using Log Analytics now that we know what is in the built-in Windows update reports.

Expanding Windows Update Reporting

We can go one step further by using Log Analytics to get more data, the ability to change it, and real-time analytics. The reports that come with Intune are great. To complete this section, we will need to create a Log Analytics area in Azure.

- Go to **https://portal.azure.com** and search for Log Analytics workspaces.
- Press "Create."
- Select the type of subscription you want, then choose or create a new Resource group.
- Give your area a name, and then click **Review** and **Create**.
- Click **Create** if everything looks good.
- Click **Monitor** when you get back to the Azure site.
- After that, go to **Workbooks** and click on **View**.
- Find Insights and click on **Windows Update for Business Reports** while scrolling down.
- Click on **Get Started**.
- Select your subscription and the area you made earlier, and then click **Save Settings.**
- To be sure, click **Save**.
- You will be notified when this is done.

The file will have data that you can change and export after a few days.

Transferring Diagnostics to Azure for Advanced Analysis

As a last note, this section also uses Azure, but this time to store Intune logs and diagnostic data in some different places, which are shown below:

- A Log Analytics workspace
- Azure Blob storage
- An event hub
- A partner solution

Because it has more features than Blob storage, we are going to use a Log Analytics area in this case.

Getting ready

We will need a Log Analytics workspace for this one. However, this one will cost money, so make sure you set up a cost alert if you launch it and then forget about it. In the Azure portal, select **Log Analytics workspace** and press create new. Create your workspace and make a note of the name. Within the **rg-loganalytics** resource group, we built an area called **intunealerts** in this case. We can set up the data to export to our desktop now that we have it.

To set up the diagnostics to export, do these things:

- Go back to the **Intune console** and click on **Reports**. Then click on **Diagnostic Settings.**
- Click on **Add diagnostic setting**.
- You can choose what to send to the area on the next screen. Keep in mind that there are fees for data, so figure out how much data you need and compare it to the possible fees. The following information can be added to your workspace:
  - **Audit Logs:** These record any changes or additions made to the Intune site, like adding new policies or deleting old ones.
  - **Operational Logs:** Enrollment of users and devices, as well as devices that don't follow the rules
  - **DeviceComplianceOrg:** Reports on device compliance and makes a list of devices that don't follow the rules.
  - **Devices**: Device inventory and status
- Check **Send to Log Analytics** workspace after choosing the reports, and then choose the workspace that you made earlier.
- Click **Save** once you're done.
- Your logs will show up in **Log Analytics under Logs** after a while.

The Configure Intune Diagnostic Data Exports section is now complete.

CHAPTER 15

PACKAGE YOUR WINDOWS APPS

We will now talk about the different kinds of applications that are out there and how to set them up in your environment. Applications are very important for handling Windows devices, and making sure they are packaged properly will make sure end users have a good experience.

Assigning applications

The assignment choices are the same for all types of apps, so we need to look at them too. We can do one of these three things:

- **Required**: This will cause an installation. It will only show up in the Company Portal under Installed Applications.
- **Available for enrolled devices**: For devices that have been enrolled, this shows the app in the Company Portal so users can do it themselves.
- **Uninstall**: This gets rid of the app.

As a general rule, set up Microsoft Entra groups for both installation and removal of apps that isn't needed across the estate. However, assignments rely on the app. This gives you more options after release, and it's especially helpful if you need to quickly get rid of an app because the group is already set up and ready to go. During assignment, you can also set a due date for installation, a delay time for restarting, and whether to show or hide the install/uninstall alerts. Another thing to think about is the person vs. device environment, especially when launching Win32 apps.

How to Utilize Microsoft Store Integration

The first thing we'll look at is the Microsoft Store integration. This no longer uses Microsoft Store for Business, but instead connects straight to the Winget store source. This is also how Windows programs like Notepad and Calculator are put in use and kept up to date. **NOTE:** Store apps that are set up through Intune will still get updates even if end users can't access the Windows Store because of a safety measure. The good news is that this change has also made it easier to launch an app!

How to do it...

- Click Apps and then Windows to start.
- Press "Add."
- Pick the Microsoft Store app (new) from the drop-down menu. It may also be called the Microsoft Store app. Then click Select.
- Open the Microsoft Store app and click Search.
- Explore the fly-out and look for the app you want to use.

NOTE: Because Intune is used a lot in schools, it will only look for apps that have a rating that is appropriate for kids. This means that some apps might not be shown.

Find these apps in the Microsoft Store online and write down the App ID, which is shown in the next picture by a red rectangle:

ID, look for that ID in Intune:

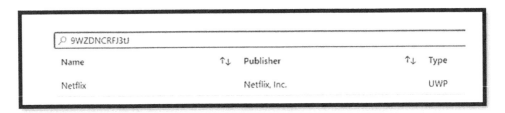

- We will keep things simple in this case and set up Company Portal because we will need it later for the exercise. Press **"Select."**
- The type will be shown as UWP by the way. There are different types of Universal Windows Platform apps, like APPX, MSIX, and more. This one is a normal store app.
- There are also a few Win32 apps that can be distributed this way instead of being put together in a Win32 intunewin program.
- Now, the information will be filled in for you (except for the logo at the time of writing). To add a logo, click "Select image" and post one.
- This is what the customer will see if they self-service install, so you can change any of the information here.

From the choices you have, these three stand out as important:

- **Show this as a featured app in Company Portal**: This will make the app stay on the Apps page in Company Portal's home screen.
- **Install behavior**: Please change this to System if you want to stop ESP until this app is installed. If not, User will work fine.

NOTE: Putting user and system in the same app can mess up your environment, so pick them out early in the deployment process.

Category: If you have a lot of apps, putting them into groups may help your users find the right one to deploy.

- Once you're sure about the information, click **Next**.
- On the Scope Tags page, click **Next**.

Take a look at the assignment now. Because we want all users to have this app, we're going to make it a required installation for the Intune Users group. After setting up, click Next.

Last, make sure everything looks good, and then click **Create**. Now we have used the UI to launch a Microsoft Store app.

Getting Started with Packaging into MSIX

MSIX is a relatively new package format. It works by keeping an eye on the installation of an application, tracking any changes to the filesystem, registry, and other areas, and then collecting these changes into a single file that can be loaded at the user level. One good thing about MSIX is that you can use it as AppAttach on Azure Virtual Desktop settings to give users access to apps without having to install them on the host machine in a multi-user setting. **NOTE**: The end user can undo changes made to an MSIX package. Do not package any programs that have databases because undoing changes will erase any changes made. It's fine to have client-server apps, but not ones that have databases built in.

Getting started

For MSIX packages to work, the following must be true:

- **Code signing certificate**: Before they can be sent out, all items must be signed. You can either buy a public code signing certificate that will be accepted by all devices immediately, or you can create a self-signing certificate and distribute it to your devices using Intune or a certificate authority (CA). To find Connectors and tokens in Intune, go to Tenant Management and click on it.

Choose your certificate and share it in Windows Enterprise Certificate.

- **Packaging machine**: If you want to package on MSIX, you will need a virtual machine. This should be as clear as possible so that you don't have to go through any extra steps that end up adding to your final package. Also, make sure that backups and checkpoints are turned on so that you can quickly use them again for the next package.

A Windows 10 or 11 computers with Hyper-V can be set up with Quick Create, which will do the following:

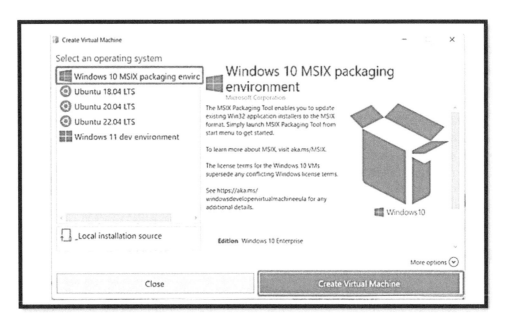

Now that the four things we need are in place, we can begin the section. First, we will package the app, and then we will look at how to deploy it.

Packaging

We can start the packaging and deployment process now that we have a machine for packaging and a license. Notepad++ will be used in this case. To prepare your first MSIXL, do these things.

- Open the **MSIX Packaging Tool** and click on **Application Package.**
- Select **Create package on this computer** and then click **Next**.
- Some checks will be done on your machine. For the best packing experience, uncheck everything that has been suggested by clicking "Disable selected" next to the item that has been marked. After that, click **Next**:

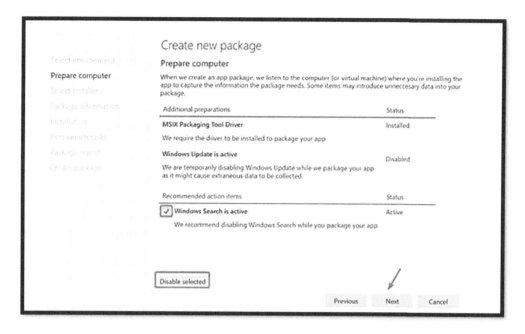

- If you know the exact steps to install, you can type them in on the next screen. We will do a full install from scratch in this case, though, so we will leave the installer boxes blank.
- This is where we will sign our application. Select **Sign with a certificate (.pfx),** point to the created certificate, and enter the password.

NOTE: It's important to fill out the Timestamp server URL box. If you don't fill this out, you will have to renew your items with a new ticket when your current one runs out. You can choose a date server, and the app will still work even after the certificate has expired as long as the certificate was still good when the app was made and signed. After putting in the information, as shown in the image below, click next:

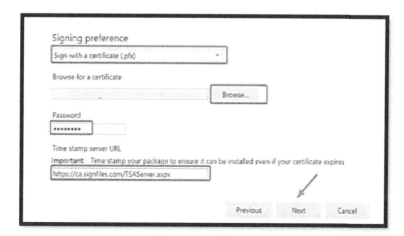

- You need to put the package information on the next screen, which says "Package information." As a general rule, app name, OS, and version are good starting points for names (for example, **Notepad++_x64_8.5.8_001**). Type in the package's **name**, its **display name**, and its **description**. These will show up in the company portal. Pick out a name for your Publisher and a version. After that, click Next.
- Install your app on the screen that says **"Create new package."** If you need to restart it, click the "Restart machine" button. The sequencer will load again when the computer starts up.
- Users can undo a package that will remove any updates, so it's a good idea to turn off automatic updates whenever possible.
- After setting up, click Next.
- The executables that have been found are shown on the next screen. Any changes made on the first run will be found by the main launcher, which can then turn off updates, hints and tips, and other things.
- You can also get rid of any executable stubs, like uninstall.exe, that you don't want users to see.
- You can click Browse and add them here by hand if any are missing. Click Next when you're done.
- Since this is the last step in tracking, you need to confirm that you still want to watch the device. Click "Yes" and go.
- You can choose to leave out any services that the sequencer found here. Click Next when you're done.
- Finally, choose where you want to save the package and click "Create." You can also get to the package builder from this page if you need to look at the files and registry keys or make more changes.

The next step is to deploy the MSIX file.

Deploying our MSIX package

We can deploy the app to Intune now that it has been packaged:

- In **Intune**, go to **Apps** and then **Windows**.
- Press "**Add**."
- Pick the **Line-of-Business** app and click "**Select**."
- Click **Select app package** file and choose the **MSIX** file that you made in the previous section. After that, click **OK**.
- You can change any information and add a picture if needed, then click **Next**.
- On the Scope Tags page, click **Next**.

Because this app is easy for people to handle themselves, we will create required and Uninstall groups to help people figure out if they need or don't need the app. These groups will then be open to everyone. This is also where you can change between downloading as a person and as a device. Once you're done setting up your assignments, click Next.

- Last, make sure everything looks good, and then click **Create**.

This is the end of the section on packing an MSIX application. The next thing we can look at is Win32 applications.

Packaging Win32 applications

This section is important to read because packaging your app into Win32 will be the main way you deploy it.

Getting started

So that we can easily figure out what's what when we need to update that weird and wonderful app in two years, we need to clean up our application source code before we do any packaging. **NOTE:** The package tool will grab all the files in the Source directory you give it, so make sure that the directory only has source files. If you point it at your Downloads folder, for example, you will wonder why a 2 MB program appears to be 45 GB when packed! Intunewin files, which are essentially encrypted ZIP files that are uploaded to Azure Blob storage along with a manifest, are created by the package tool. When you say "install," your computer gets, decrypts, and runs the software file.

This is completely up to you, but this way of organizing folders works well:

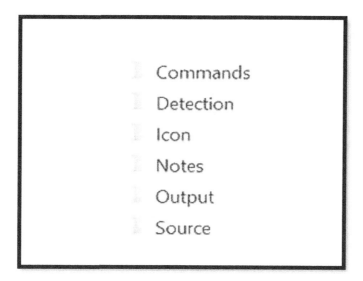

The raw files, launcher and configuration files, and other files can be found in the Source folder. The intunewin file will be saved in output. The rest should be pretty clear. Don't forget to save a copy of any source files you use because you can't get them back once you add them to Intune. Now it's time to look at the different ways to make an installer.

Calling MSI/Exe directly

It would be easy to just package the MSI or executable file by itself, and then we could tell Intune to run the file during the installation:

- *msiexec.exe /i myinstaller.msi /qn myinstaller.exe /silent*

This is fine, but it doesn't let you make any changes before or after the installation. Also, keep in mind that Intune may make the MSI install in the user context if that's how it was written. You'll know this because the context will be grayed out. You will need to change the MSI or find a way to wrap it if you want one of these to run in the system context.

Batch script

It is much more current and powerful to use PowerShell, but a batch script will still work for packing. If this is what makes you feel better, that's fine. **PowerShell or the PowerShell Application Deployment Toolkit (PSADT)** might be a better choice in the long run, but for now, this will do just fine.

Create a batch script for installation. This is your install file when you package:

For example:
rem Delete file
del c:\temp\myfile.txt
rem Stop Service
net stop myservice
rem Install App
my-installer.exe /verysilent /allusers /noreboot
rem Delete Shortcut
del %public%\desktop\myshortcut.lnk

Here are some helpful tips for people who use batch scripts.

Type SET at a command window to see a list of the machine's settings. You can link to these inside%, as we did with the public user environment, %public%. **You don't need to add a backslash when you talk about the current directory:**

%~dp0myinstaller.exe

Just change the install command in Intune to install.bat or whatever you named your batch script.

PowerShell script

PowerShell scripts give you more power over the machine, which makes installation even better. It's also easier to do tricky things with them. Anything is possible at this point. You can add code and look at the hardware underneath.

In this case, the following code must be run in a PowerShell script for it to run an MSI:

$MSIArguments = @(
"/i"
('"{0}"' -f $filelocation)
"/qn"
"/norestart"
*"/L*v"*
)
Start-Process "msiexec.exe" -ArgumentList $MSIArguments -Wait -NoNewWindow

- You can, of course, add or remove features for apps that don't have an MSI when you use PowerShell.

We'll use DotNet as an example here:

- *Enable-WindowsOptionalFeature -Online -FeatureName 'NetFx3' -Source .\sxs\ -NoRestart -LimitAccess*

This is what the installation command in Intune would look like:

- *powershell.exe -ExecutionPolicy Bypass -file myinstaller.ps1*

PSADT

PSADT (https://psappdeploytoolkit.com/) is a very powerful tool that works with PowerShell and has a lot of extra features that can be used to make the process even better. Check to see if any programs are open and ask the user to close them if they are, run a certain file in the user context while the rest run in the system context, or add tasks before and after installation. **NOTE:** If you want users to be able to interact with your app after deployment through Intune, you will need to use the ServiceUI application from Microsoft

Deployment Tools (MDT) toolkit

The following would be the install code for deploying a PSADT-packaged program that allows users to interact with it:

- *.\ServiceUI.exe -Process:explorer.exe Deploy-Application.exe*

We've talked about the different ways to install an app, so now we can talk about how to package one.

How to do it…

We need to use Microsoft's IntuneWinAppUtil to package our source files and launcher now that we have them. This opens and bundles the source files and gives us the intunewinfile.

If you want to package your app in intunewin format, do these things:

- First, we need to load the app. To make things easier, we'll use 7-Zip. A message will ask us to name the source folder.
- Point it at the Source folder, which has your software media and setup file and was made earlier.
- After that, type in the name of the application file (setup file).
- The last step is to tell **IntuneWinAppUtil** to put the intunewin file (in the Output folder).
- We need to figure out how Intune can tell that the download was successful once the app has been packaged.

Application detection

Before you add something to Intune, you should get the detection type to let it know that the download went well.

To find our sensor and then set it up in Intune, we can follow these steps:

Most of the time, Windows Sandbox can be used as a test machine to look for a file or registry key that can be used to identify something. And if you have an MSI app, you can quickly get the product code with this PowerShell script:

$path = "PATH TO MSI"
$comObjWI = New-Object -ComObject WindowsInstaller.Installer $MSIDatabase =
$comObjWI.GetType().InvokeMember("OpenDatabase
","InvokeMethod",$Null,$comObjWI,@($Path,0)) $Query = "SELECT Value FROM Property
WHERE Property = 'ProductCode'" $View =
$MSIDatabase.GetType().InvokeMember("OpenView"
,"InvokeMethod",
$null,$MSIDatabase,($Query))
$View.GetType().InvokeMember("Execute",
"InvokeMethod", $null, $View, $null)
$Record =
$View.GetType().InvokeMember("Fetch","InvokeMe thod",$null,$View,$null) $Value =
$Record.GetType().InvokeMember("StringData","G etProperty",$null,$Record,1)
write-host "Your MSI code is $Value" - ForegroundColor Green

This script will give you the MSI code that you can use for both detection and uninstallation.

We need to add the file to Intune now that we have it.

- Go to the Intune site and click on **Apps**. Then click on **Windows**.
- Click **Add** after that.
- Choose **Windows app (Win32)** from the drop-down menu and click **Select**.

- Click on the blue text that says **"Select app package file."**
- Now, navigate to the Intunewin file we made earlier, and then click OK.
- Since we packed an application, it will only fill in the path, so we need to add a publisher at the very least and a name, description, version, and image at the very best. After you've filled out these forms, click **Next**.

On the next screen, we can change a few things. To begin, fill in the **Install and Uninstall** instructions, based on how the app was packed. This could be a PowerShell or batch script, or it could just be a file path. Both areas should be filled in automatically if the app is an MSI.

- You can also choose how long the process should go on before it stops and says it failed. This works better for bigger or more complicated tasks. The usual setting of 60 minutes will work fine for 7-Zip.
- **Allow available uninstall** is for apps that users can install themselves through the Company Portal. By setting this to "Yes," they will also be able to uninstall the app on their own.
- The action that this app installs needs to be set to **System**. But some apps may be built on users, so change this as needed.
- You can also tell it what to do to restart if it needs to.
- Finally, add any strange return codes that the app has here. Most of the time, the usual codes will work fine.
- Click **Next** when you're done.
- Next, we need to set the system conditions so that the app can be installed. The software will not go further if a device does not meet these requirements.

At the device level, you can set more specifics, such as the RAM and processor speed for more complicated programs like CAD software. You can also add your own needs script if you want to go even further. As an example, if you only want to install on laptops (for a VPN client), you could use the **Windows Management Interface (WMI)** to ask about the device chassis and then ask about that here.

- For 7-Zip, we only need to make sure the computer is 64-bit because that's the version we've sent you. After setting up, click Next.
- The next step is to set up the recognition rule. This is what Intune will use to make sure the app is installed properly.

We can do a few things here:

- **MSI:** This will be filled in automatically for any straight MSI files. A **globally unique identity (GUID)** for MSI can also be added. This will check to see if that ID is already there.
- **File:** Look for a certain file by name, date, version, or size (this is helpful for updates). One thing you could do is point it to the file that is run. Take note of the 32/64-bit choice. If you choose "Yes," it will look in the 32-bit context on 64-bit computers, like in Program Files (x86).

- **Registry**: In the register, look for a certain key, word, version, or number. It's the same for 32-bit and 64-bit.
- **Requirements script**: This script lets you look for almost anything, like a service that is working or a mix of different ways. To make this work, the script needs to end with an exit code of 0, which means it worked. This can be seen in this case:

```
$service = get-service -name
"MozillaMaintenance"
if ($service.Status -eq "Running") { write-output "MozillaMaintenance
detected and running, exiting"
exit 0
}
else {
exit 1
}
```

- For 7-Zip, we will use a File Rule type with the right path and file set to check for the presence of the 7z program.
- Click Next when we're done setting up the detection.
- The next section will talk about Dependencies and Supersedence, so we can press Next on these two for now.
- On the Scope Tags page, click Next.
- It's time to give the application to someone. For better control, we will set Available for registered devices to All Users (or All Devices) since this is free software. However, we will make sure that Required and Uninstall are set to specific groups. After setting up, click Next:

Managing App Supersedence and Dependencies

In this section, we'll look at how application supersedence and application dependencies work. We will not talk about automating because it includes changing current apps. Instead, we will talk about why you would use these and how to set them up.

Application supersedence

When a new version of an app comes out, you can do one of a few things:

- Get a new IntuneWin file and change the way it finds things so it works with the current version.
- Make a new app and switch the assignments around.
- Use the application supersedence

You can choose to remove the old version before downloading the new one or just do an update. Everything will still work fine. Because you won't have to worry about giving out the same assignment twice or keeping track of multiple applications, it's also easier to handle.

Dependencies

One problem with Intune and Autopilot is that they can't put apps in order like Configuration Manager can. Hence, in the past, you couldn't be sure that a program that needed a certain engine (.NET, Java, VC Libraries, etc.) would be installed in time if it needed to start. Before dependencies, this meant you had to bundle them both into one app and then install it to use the install script. This worked well, but every time you updated one of the apps, you had to re-package both of them, even if only one had changed. This is where a dependency comes in handy: you pick the code or app that you need and make it a dependency on the main app. Then, Intune will check to see if the app is already loaded. If it isn't, it will install the dependency first, and then launch the main app.

Getting started

You will need the following to follow this section:

- The same application for supersedence in two different versions
- An application that has a dependency

Starting with application supersedence, we can now examine the steps involved in creating these settings.

Configuring application supersedence

We will use 7-Zip and change version 19.00 to 23.00 for this case. To set up application supersedence in the application setup, do the following:

- Click on **Apps** first, then **Windows**.
- Look through the list to find your application. New versions can be used to replace old ones. In our case, 7-Zip 23.00 is needed. Press on it.
- Press on **Properties**.
- Find "**Supersedence**" and click "**Edit**."
- Click "**+Add**" to add the app that it will replace.
- In the fly-out, find the app you want to use and click **Select**.
- If you have to completely remove the old version of the app before you can load the new one, set **Uninstall to Yes**. When everything is right, click **Review + Save.**
- Finally, click "**Save**" to make sure the changes are saved.

If you are confident that the new version does not need any extra testing, this can also be set up during the initial application release. By configuring it after release, you can check the new version for bugs before releasing it. Let's learn how to configure application dependency now that we've talked about supersedence.

Configuring application dependency

We will be setting the Visual C++ 2013 Redistributable package as a dependency for our new 7-Zip 23.00 version, even though it is not required.

To set up our app's dependency on other apps, follow these steps:

- Click on **Apps** first, then **Windows**.
- Look for your app in the list—in this case, 7-Zip 23.00—and click on it.
- Press on **Properties**.
- Click **Edit** after scrolling down to **Dependencies**.
- Click "**+ Add**" to bring up a menu with a list of applications.
- Look for your app in the list, click on it, and then click "**Select**."

You can choose here whether you want the app to install itself when the parent app is installed or if you want to do it yourself. The better choice most of the time is automatic. Click **Review + Save** when you're done setting up everything.

- If you set up any supersedences, you will be asked to confirm them here. We already know these are right, so click **Review + Save** again.
- Finally, click **Save** to confirm your changes to the application.

What are application supersedence and application dependencies? We now know what they are and how to set them up for tenant applications.

Deploying Office Applications

Another name for the Microsoft Office Suite of Apps is Microsoft 365 Apps. It's likely one of the most important apps you need on your devices. We need to make sure they are set up properly, regularly, and ideally forced on the Enrollment Status Page (ESP) because of this.

Getting started

There are three different ways to install Microsoft 365 apps in Intune. One of them is much more reliable than the other two. Using the **Office Deployment Tool** (**ODT**) to wrap it as a Win32 app is the best way to do it. As we can then control how it is deployed during the ESP, we will discuss this in this section. We also know that the **Intune Management Extension (IME)**, which keeps apps from fighting, will be used to install it. We should look at the other options on the site before we look at how to launch as a Win32 application.

These are using the graphical user interface (GUI) with setup creator choices or by entering XML:

- Click on **Apps** first, then **Windows**.
- Click **Add**, and then pick **Microsoft 365 Apps for Windows 10 and later.** Click **Select**.
- At the first screen, click "**Next**." This will take you to the "Configure app suite" screen.

You can quickly set up your application package with the Configuration Designer tool, which doesn't require you to change any XML or package any apps. It is a quick way to launch the apps, but since you don't have any more control, you can't say which apps, like Skype for Business, should not be installed. You don't have much control over this. You can use unique XML made by the Office Customization Tool when you switch to Enter XML data, which is what we will do for the Win32 program. There is a chance that the built-in Microsoft 365 application setup will conflict with another version if you use it. This is because it is installed more as a strategy than an application. Detection, specific needs, supersedence, and dependencies (which are helpful if you have apps that install Office tools) are also out of your hands.

How to do it...

Let us learn how to set up, package, and deploy a program as a Win32 application now that we've looked at the methods we should not use. **If you want to use Office as a Win32 program, follow these steps:**

- Setting up our XML file is the first thing we need to do. This will tell the Office Deployment Tool what languages to use, which components to load, and so on. Go to the **Office Customization Tool** to do that.

You can choose which version of Office to run, which programs to get rid of, which language packs to use, and more here. We will be configuring the update channel using Intune in the next section, so when specifying the update channel here, ideally, it should match your **Broad Ring** to save users from downgrading after installation. You can also specify which version to install should you have specific application requirements.

- In the **Installation** choices, it's best to keep **Show installation to user** set to **No**, since this will be running in the system context anyway. Also, make sure that **Shut down running apps** is set to **Yes** if you are launching during Autopilot. If something is already running, you might have timeout problems. It might be better to use **PSADT** and tell users to close the apps themselves if you are launching after the initial setup since you can't be sure when the app will be deployed.

Keep an eye on the **"Uninstall any MSI versions of Office,"** which can be found in the "**Update and upgrade**" menu. This will get rid of any Office programs that were found. This probably won't be a problem if you're installing the whole suite, but if you're installing apps one at a time, like **Visio or Project**, make sure this is set to No. If it's not, it will remove everything except the app you chose to install. First, go to Licensing and Activation and change Automatically Accept the EULA to Yes. This way, your end users won't have to accept it themselves.

When it comes to licensing, we have three main choices:

- **User-based**: Each user is given a license, and they can only have five installs before the Office site asks them to remove a permitted installation.
- **Shared Computer**: This choice works best in places where employees can use a lot of different devices, like hospitals or hot desks. One of the five licenses for users will not be used by a device that is set to "Shared Computer" mode. Make sure that your rights allow this choice if you want to use it.
- **Device-based**: It's the machine itself that's licensed when it has multiple unauthorized users. This needs a special permit.

You can set up anything that can be handled by Group Policy or Intune Policy in **Application Preferences.** This works fine for one-time settings, but using Intune policies will give you more freedom and let you make changes without having to re-package apps.

- Click **Export** once you've finished adjusting your settings.
- Select the style you want for the file, click "OK," and then save the XML.
- We need a way to use our XML file to bring the Office apps to users now that we have it. The Office Deployment Tool will be used for this. You can move the files into a folder by running the software file that you downloaded.

Now we must create the folder structure for Win32. You can get the XML file and setup.exe file from the Office Deployment Tool and put them in the Source folder.

Create a uninstall.xml file with the following information as well:

<Configuration>
<Display Level="None" AcceptEULA="True" />
<Property Name="FORCEAPPSHUTDOWN" Value="True"
/>
<Remove>
<Product ID="O365ProPlusRetail">
</Product>
</Remove>
</Configuration>

Use the IntuneWinAppUtil tool to wrap it, choose setup.exe as the installer, and save intunewin in the Output folder. We can add our IntuneWin file to Intune now that we have it.

- Go to Apps and then Windows in the Intune site.
- Click "Add," pick "Win32," and click "Select."
- Click the folder icon, grab your intunewin file, and click OK.

Everything needs to be filled in since this is a Win32 app from a file. This includes the icon. After setting up, click Next. Now we need to say how to install and remove.

For your install command, you need the following: ***setup.exe /configure Configuration.xml***
For the uninstall command, you need this: ***setup.exe /configure uninstall.xml***
- Any other settings can be made, then click **Next**.
- We set our software to 64-bit, so make that the condition along with the newest version of Windows in your estate. After that, click **Next**.
- It can be harder to set detection rules for Office programs because they install the Click-To-Run program first, which then downloads the files. We will now look for a registry key that will let us know the Click-To-Run tool is no longer working. These are the registry keys that we have set up:

Key Path:
HKEY_LOCAL_MACHINE\SOFTWARE\Microsoft\Offi ce\ClickToRun
Value: LastScenarioResult
Detection: Exists
- Since we're deploying the 32-bit version, we don't want to link it to a 32-bit app. If we do, it will try to connect to WOW6432Node and fail the recognition process. Set **Associated with a 32-bit app on 64-bit clients** to **No**.
- Once everything is set up, click OK and then Next.
- This app is a key app that is needed across the estate, so there are no Dependencies, Supersedence, or Scope tags for it. Click Next on all three screens.
- You can choose **All Users, All Devices**, or **Deploy to a Group** when looking at assignments. You will undoubtedly want this installed on all devices. Click **Next** once you've chosen the group.

- Finally, check the **Review + Create** screen to make sure that everything we set up is correct, then click **Create**.

This is the end of the section on deploying Microsoft 365 apps. Let's find out how to keep the apps up to date.

Updating Office Applications

We need to make sure that our Office apps stay up to date now that they are deployed. Because these are key apps, it's best to use the same ring method we used for Windows updates. This way, you can check for problems with the business and for big changes to the user interface that might need to be shared with the company. There are several ways to handle Office updates, and this article will go over the best one. We will first look at the two main choices and then go over how to set them up.

Office portal

One choice is to use the Office Admin site. Here, you can set any setup setting for Office policies through **Policy Management**. You can also use the **Cloud Updates** menu to handle updates and version releases. This is a good choice, but because it's not part of the Intune portal, it's an extra portal to keep track of and there's a higher chance of problems because the same setting could be set up in two places.

Settings catalog

We can change any ADMX-backed settings directly on the devices using the Settings catalog, and we can use our current update groups or create new ones. In this section, we will do this.

Office updates

- Go to **Devices**, click on **Windows**, and then click on **Configuration Profiles**. This is the same as all the other recipes that use the Settings library.
- At the top, click **Create**. Then, choose **New Policy**. Next, choose **Windows 10 and later**. Finally, choose the Settings **catalog** from the window that pops up. Last, click on **Create**.
- Give your new page a name and a description. Choose names for the rings that reflect the fact that you will need at least three different profiles for them in most situations. After that, click Next.
- Click **Add Settings** on the **Settings** page, then find **Microsoft Office 2016 (Machine)** in the list. Click on **Updates**. The policies for Office 2016 are the most up-to-date and work with all Microsoft 365 tools.
- Users cannot change their update frequency by selecting the machine policies, which write the keys to **HKEY Local Machine (HKLM)** rather than the **HKEY Current User (HKCU) hive.**

- **We need these two settings for updates:**
  - **Enable Automatic Updates**: Set to **Enabled**.
  - **Update Channel:** Make sure it's turned on. Set Channel to match the ring that is being set up.
- If you need to, you can also change the **Update Deadline** in the settings section.
- Once you've picked the right channel, click "**Next**."
- Click **Next** to go to the next page after the **Scope tags** page.

Now, assign the application. For Office updates, the set of users and devices may be different, so you might want to put some heavy Office app users in one of the earlier rings to find any problems quickly before they are rolled out to the rest of the estate. If your users often switch between computers, like IT staff, you might want to use device groups to stop Office versions from upgrading and downgrading as different users log in. Just be careful not to mix device and user groups when adding and removing groups.

- Click **Next** when you're done setting up your assignments.
- Finally, check to make sure everything is right, and then click **Create**.

The configuration of Office updates in the UI is now complete.

Windows Application Protection

Application protection is more crucial than ever because more users are viewing work info from their own devices. **Windows Mobile Application Management (MAM)** is a new feature that only works with the Microsoft Edge browser at the time of this writing. In this method, we will set up MAM and then add **conditional access** policies to stop personal devices from accessing anything that isn't Microsoft Edge. First, keep in mind that personal devices can't sign up for Microsoft Intune. If they do, they will get around the rules for restricted access.

To set up Windows application protection, do these things:

- The first step is to make MAM work for the whole tenant. You only need to do this once.
- Go to Tenant Administration and click on Connectors and Tokens. Then click on Mobile Threat Defense.
- Add a way for the Windows Security Center to connect.

TIP: Don't worry if it says "not available"; it will update when it is used.

- Next, go to **Apps** and click on **App Protection Policies**.
- Click "**Create New**" and pick "**Windows**" instead of "Windows Information Protection."
- Give your policy a **name** and a **description**, then click "**Next**."
- Click the blue **+ Select Apps** text on the Apps screen and pick **Microsoft Edge**. After clicking **Select**, click **Next**.
- Set up your data protection settings. For example, choose whether you want to allow data to be moved into or out of the program and whether you want to make printing impossible. After that, click **Next**.

- You can set up more protection for the data on the **Health Checks** screen. For example, you can choose how many days after creation to delete the data, and you can also add minimum application versions. You can set the minimum operating system versions under "**Device conditions**" to stop any Microsoft installs that aren't allowed.

TIP: Disabled Account is a health check setting that you might want to add here. This way, you can be sure that any former workers can't get in on their own devices.

- Click **Next** when you're done setting up everything.
- Since this is a global rule, click **Next** on the Scope groups page.
- Assign tasks as needed. Keep in mind that this is happening at the user level and applies to devices that aren't signed up for **Intune or Entra ID**, so the group needs to have users in it. You could create a dynamic group with all people who have a valid Intune license, but there is currently no choice to choose all users. After setting up, click **Next**.
- Finally, make sure the settings look good and click **Create**.
- We need to add extra protection for limited access now that the Intune side has been finished.
- Go to **Endpoint security** and click on **Conditional access**.

By requiring compliance, we need to keep devices that aren't owned by the company from viewing anything but the web app. Even though you should do this on all devices, this policy only applies to BYOD, so we will also use a device filter to leave out machines that belong to the company.

First, choose **All users** (except your **Break Glass account**) and All cloud apps. We don't want any data to leave without being secure. Since this is a Windows-only setup, make sure that the device platforms are set to only Windows. We don't want this policy to apply to other platforms:

In this case, we want to let the computer through. In the next strategy, we will make sure that stays safe. So, this rule should be applied to everything except **Browser**:

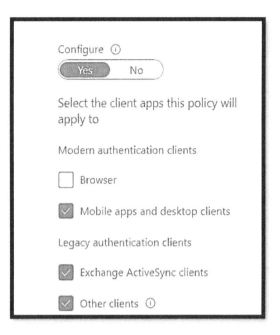

As we already said, we will leave out corporate devices by using the filter shown in the next picture:

device.deviceOwnership -eq "Company"

Then we need to require compliance, which will block devices that aren't owned by the company immediately. To do this, go to **Grant access**: click on **require device to be marked as compliant**.

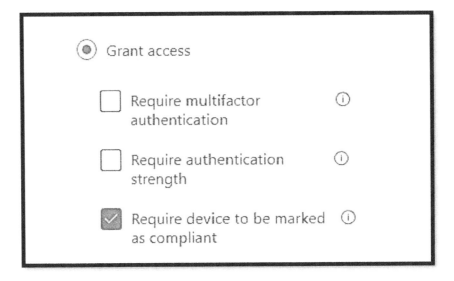

This has blocked our access that isn't through a browser. With the second restricted access strategy, we want to stop browsers from getting in. Once more, we want to reach **all users, all cloud apps** and also include only **Windows devices**. This policy should only be used on **Browser**; if you choose something else, it will fail.

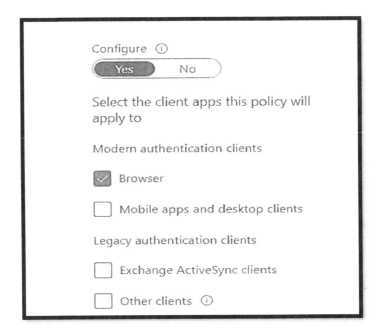

With the same filter, ignore corporate devices once more. The most important thing is that we need to **require app protection policy** under **Grant access**:

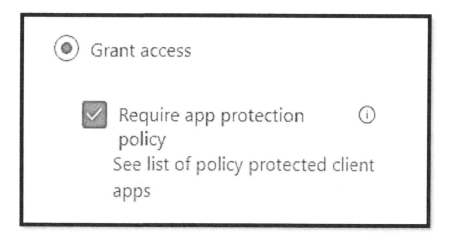

As an extra safety measure, you can also **Use Conditional Access App Control** in the **Session** settings to **block downloads (Preview):**

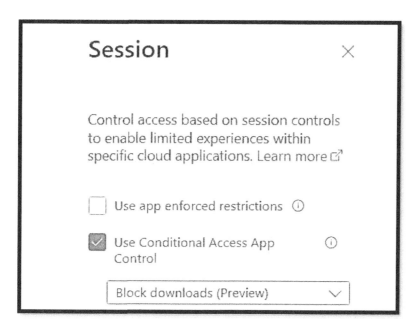

On personal devices, we have now protected our data in the Edge browser, and on Windows, we have stopped anyone from getting to it in any other way.

CHAPTER 16
TROUBLESHOOTING
Common Intune Troubleshooting Issues and Solutions

Even though Microsoft Intune has a lot of features, you might still run into problems when you use it. When you have a problem, here are some ways to solve it:

Problems with enrolling devices

One common problem with Intune is that it's hard to join devices. If a user's Azure AD join settings are wrong, security policies change or limited access rules are put in place, they may run into problems. These problems can be quickly fixed with the help of tools like the Intune device troubleshooter, logs, and Intune support files.

Mobile Device Management Troubles

Management of smart devices could be another problem. For example, IT compliance policies might not be able to be put into place because of settings that are at odds with each other, or registered devices might not be able to sync with the Intune service. To fix these Intune problems, you can take preventative steps like looking at the Event logs and checking the renter state.

Application Protection Policy Misconfiguration

Application security policies often cause problems because they are not set up correctly or people don't understand them. If you don't protect or handle data correctly, it can affect how well a service works. These Intune problems can be fixed by IT experts who change settings in the Intune site and look over application setup policies.

Connectivity and Performance Issues

Network problems or system overloads can make it hard for the Intune service to connect and work properly. Using the built-in state tracking and reporting tools in Intune can help you find these problems. These kinds of problems can be fixed by regularly updating the system and checking its performance.

Reporting and Compliance Difficulties

Businesses may also have trouble reporting compliance or going over the collected data because of mistakes in the system or data that isn't full. Using specific reporting and inspection tools that come with Microsoft Intune makes it possible to keep track of, evaluate, and fix these problems.

Authentication and Authorization Errors

Authentication and permission mistakes often happen because access policies are not set up correctly or passwords are out of date. Regular checks, reviews of IT policies, and password changes will get rid of these problems and make troubleshooting Intune easier.

Advanced Troubleshooting Techniques for Microsoft Intune

For Intune troubleshooting, you can use some more advanced techniques once you understand the basics. Taking that extra step could be the key to fixing Intune problems that won't go away.

Utilizing Microsoft Intune's Troubleshooting Portal

Microsoft Intune's Troubleshooting Portal is a powerful tool that all IT professionals should know how to use. By going to the site, you can see all the information about your device in one place. For better Intune troubleshooting, the site shows problems with device registration, policy rollout, or compliance policies.

Diagnostic Logging and Reporting

Other important parts of Intune troubleshooting are diagnostic logging and reports. Diagnostic logging tells you important things about how the system works and shows you where things went wrong. In this case, if users have recently changed security policies or had problems with entry rules, it should be clear in the log. It can also show you if there are any problems between the states of registered devices and how you think they should act. Reporting, on the other hand, fixes Intune problems by doing things before they happen. You can get ahead of problems before they hurt the user experience by tailoring reports to focus on high-priority areas like current device management. For example, a report on problems with Microsoft Edge could be set up to be checked every day. This would let you know early on about possible problems with Intune.

Regular System Updates and Upgrades

Regular changes and upgrades are important for Microsoft Intune to work well, just like they are for any other system. Updates generally fix bugs that have already been found, make the program run faster, and make it safer. If you keep up with these changes, you can save time and stress when you're troubleshooting Intune. You might want to make a plan for checking for and installing system changes. As a way to make sure users are up-to-date on the latest Intune troubleshooting methods, Microsoft often posts information on its official websites and social media accounts. As part of this, you will move from the Intune interface to the new and better Microsoft Endpoint Manager Control center.

Troubleshooting some Windows device enrollment errors in Intune

Error hr 0x8007064c: The machine is already enrolled

If you encounter an enrollment failure with the error message "The machine is already enrolled" along with error hr 0x8007064c, it may stem from various reasons, including previous enrollment, a cloned image with enrollment data, or lingering account certificates.

To resolve this issue, follow these steps:

Solution:
1. **Access MMC:**
   - Press the Windows key and type "Run" to open the Run dialog.
   - Type "**MMC**" and hit Enter.
2. **Add/Remove Snap-ins:**
   - In the MMC console, go to "**File**" and select "Add/Remove Snap-ins."
3. **Select Certificates:**
   - Double-click "Certificates" and choose "Computer account" > "Next," then select "Local Computer."
4. **Navigate to Certificates:**
   - Expand "Certificates (Local Computer)" and select "Personal" > "Certificates."
5. **Delete Intune Certificate:**
   - Locate the Intune certificate issued by Sc_Online_Issuing.
   - If found, delete it.
6. **Delete Registry Key:**
   - Check if the registry key exists: HKEY_LOCAL_MACHINE\SOFTWARE\Microsoft\OnlineManagement and delete it along with all subkeys.
7. **Re-Enroll:**
   - Attempt to re-enroll the device.
8. **Additional Steps:**
   - If the issue persists, search for and delete the registry key: KEY_CLASSES_ROOT\Installer\Products\6985F0077D3EEB44AB6849B5D7913E95.
9. **Re-Attempt Enrollment:**
   - Retry the enrollment process.

Error 8018000a: The Device is Already Enrolled

Encountering error code 8018000a, along with the message "Something went wrong. The device is already enrolled," indicates that the device has already been enrolled by a different user in Intune or joined to Microsoft Entra ID. To resolve this issue, follow these steps:

Cause:

- Another user has already enrolled the device in Intune or joined the device to Microsoft Entra ID. This can be confirmed by checking Settings > Accounts > Work Access for a message similar to "Another user on the system is already connected to a work or school. Please remove that work or school connection and try again."

Solution:

1. **Sign Out and Sign In with the Other Account:**
   - Sign out of Windows and then sign in using the account that has already enrolled or joined the device.
2. **Remove Work or School Account:**
   - Navigate to Settings > Accounts > Work Access.
   - Remove the work or school account associated with the device.
3. **Sign Out and Sign In with Your Account:**
   - Sign out of Windows and sign in again using your account.
4. **Enroll or Join the Device:**
   - Proceed to enroll the device in Intune or join the device to Microsoft Entra ID using your account.

This account is not allowed on this phone

Error: "This account is not allowed on this phone. Make sure the information you provided is correct, and then try again or request support from your company."

Cause: The user who tried to enroll the device doesn't have a valid Intune license.

Solution: Assign a valid Intune license to the user, and then enroll the device.

Looks like the MDM Terms of Use endpoint is not correctly configured

Error: MDM Terms of Use Endpoint Misconfiguration

Encountering an error indicating that the MDM Terms of Use endpoint is not correctly configured typically arises due to one of the following reasons:

Cause:

1. **User License Issue:**
   - The user attempting to enroll the device lacks a valid Intune license or an Office 365 license.
   - This scenario triggers an error message stating, "Looks like we can't connect to the URL for your organization's MDM terms of use."
2. **Incorrect MDM Terms and Conditions URL:**
   - The MDM terms and conditions URL within Microsoft Entra ID is either empty or does not contain the correct URL.

Solution: To resolve this issue, you can implement one of the following methods:

1. **Assign a Valid License to the User:**
   - Go to the Microsoft 365 Admin Center and assign either an Intune or a Microsoft 365 license to the user.

2. **Correct the MDM Terms of Use URL:**
   - Sign in to the Azure portal and navigate to Microsoft Entra ID.
   - Select "Mobility (MDM and MAM)" and click on "Microsoft Intune."
   - Choose "Restore default MDM URLs" and ensure that the MDM terms of use URL are set to https://portal.manage.microsoft.com/TermsofUse.aspx.
   - Click "Save" to apply the changes.

Something went wrong

Encountering error code 80180026 typically occurs when attempting to join a Windows 10 computer to Microsoft Entra ID under the following conditions:

Cause:
- MDM automatic enrollment is enabled in Azure.
- The Intune PC software client (Intune PC agent) is installed on the Windows 10 computer.

Solution:
To resolve this issue, you can utilize one of the following methods:
1. **Disable MDM Automatic Enrollment in Azure:**
   1. Sign in to the Azure portal.
   2. Navigate to Microsoft Entra ID > Mobility (MDM and MAM) > Microsoft Intune.
   3. Set MDM User scope to None.
   4. Click "Save" to apply the changes.
2. **Uninstall the Intune Client:**
   - Uninstall the Intune PC software client agent from the affected Windows 10 computer.

Error: "The Software Cannot Be Installed, 0x80cf4017"

Encountering error code 0x80cf4017, accompanied by the message "The software cannot be installed," typically indicates that the client software is out of date.

Cause:
- The client software version is outdated, leading to installation failure.

Solution:
To resolve this issue, follow these steps:
1. **Sign in to the Admin Portal:**
   - Visit https://admin.manage.microsoft.com.
2. **Download Client Software:**
   - Navigate to Admin > Client Software Download.
   - Click on "Download Client Software."
3. **Save and Install the Package:**
   - Save the installation package to your device.
   - Execute the installation process for the client software.

Error: "The Account Certificate is Not Valid and May be Expired, 0x80cf4017"

Encountering error code 0x80cf4017, accompanied by the message "The account certificate is not valid and may be expired," also indicates an issue related to outdated client software.

Cause:
- Similar to the previous error, the client software version is outdated, leading to the certificate validity issue.

Solution:
Follow the same steps provided above to resolve this issue:
1. **Sign in to the Admin Portal:**
   - Visit https://admin.manage.microsoft.com.
2. **Download Client Software:**
   - Navigate to Admin > Client Software Download.
   - Click on "Download Client Software."
3. **Save and Install the Package:**
   - Save the installation package to your device.
   - Execute the installation process for the client software.

CHAPTER 17

FREQUENTLY ASKED QUESTIONS (INTUNE INTERVIEW QUESTIONS AND ANSWERS)

Note: These Intune Interview questions must be treated as **Intune FAQs** or Frequently Asked Questions. You will get all the details if you go through the questions and associated links in each question.

How can I sign up for a Microsoft Intune free trial account?

You have to set up a Microsoft Intune tenant before you can sign up for a free trial account. You can use the Intune portal for free for 30 days if you don't already have access to it. You can sign in and add Intune to your contract with the account you used to access the sample, whether it's from work or school. If not, you can make a new account to use with Intune.

What information is required to fill up the sign-up form for Microsoft Intune free trial?

People who want to try Microsoft Intune for free must give their email address, name, business phone number, company name, and size, country or area, and the domain name that your business or group uses.

What should I do after filling up the sign-up form for Microsoft Intune free trial?

After completing the sign-up form, you must click "**Next**," confirm your phone number by entering the code sent to your mobile device, choose a domain name and username, create a password, give some basic information about the user account, and, if asked, enter your tax ID or PAN registration number.

What can I do after successfully creating a Microsoft Intune trial account?

You can access the Microsoft 365 admin Center, set up your property, add users and groups, give licenses, control users and groups, see information about your contract, and start the modern endpoint management process once you've successfully created a Microsoft Intune trial account. You can also help users and other devices, and if needed, you can add apps to start the modern endpoint control process.

Who manages Intune Version Upgrades?

Software as a Service, or SaaS, is what Intune does. Microsoft is in charge of updating or upgrading the hardware of Intune servers. Intune Manager doesn't have to worry about setting up infrastructure, updating versions, and other things. These are run by Microsoft engineers.

Is there any need for server installation for Intune?

Intune doesn't need any computer hardware to work like on-premise systems do. Since Intune is a SaaS service, Microsoft is in charge of all the computer technology and design. For certificate profile distribution, however, the server infrastructure might be needed to support some extra features, like an NDES connection, among other things. But once more, these are not Intune parts.

What are the Intune Architecture and Design Decisions?

It's getting harder to figure out the answer to this question. Like most device control apps, Intune is made up of a computer and a client. Intune Service is what runs on the computer. There are two parts to the client side.

- Windows MDM Client (built-in to OS)
- Intune Management Extension (IME) agent

The architecture and design choices for Intune (the cloud) are very different from those for on-premise device control systems like SCCM. When you make decisions about planning and style, you should keep the SaaS option in mind.

- You don't have to make any choices about where to put Intune servers or how to build the core Intune infrastructure components. Apple has already taken care of this. Their **Azure Datacenter**s and computers are spread out across all regions.
- Decisions need to be made about how to connect networks to Intune services from on-premises and the Internet. In this case, endpoint devices connect from the on-premises network to the cloud, and administrators connect from the on-premises network to Intune services.

For organizations to add new and current devices to Intune control using Windows Autopilot/ADE, they may need a separate network just for registration.

- Decisions must be made about how to design approved registration options for the company. How about this: Do you only want to support Apple ADE, Android Device Admin, or Windows Autopilot enrollments?
- Use Intune to make design decisions about applications, policies, Windows updates, updates for third-party apps, and certificate distribution methods. Strategies for packing (MSIX) and repackaging (IntuneWin), among other things.

- The plans for distributing content with **Delivery Optimization (DO)** for both on-premises and home networks. Set up the device control life cycle with Intune as well.
- One of the most important design decisions was how to connect Intune to current environments like ServiceNow, SCCM, and others.

What types of devices can be managed with Intune?

The list of device platforms with Intune support is increasing day by day. The types of device platforms which can be enrolled are as follows:

- **Windows**
- **Android**
- **iOS/iPadOS**
- **macOS**
- **Linux**

Where to check the status of Intune service?

The **Intune Tenant Admin–Tenant status** tab in the Intune admin portal can be used to see what the current state of the Intune is.

Where can you check Intune Version Details?

The Intune (also called "Intune admin") portal is where you can find out about the different versions of Intune. You can find the Service Release number by going to the **Intune Portal**, then **Tenant Administration.**

What is Device Enrollment in Intune context?

Adding desktops and mobile devices to a company's MDM system, like Intune, is called "**device enrollment.**" There are different ways to sign up for something. The process for setting up a device is different for each OS. Each registration method would have a different setup and user experience. During the registration process, an **MDM certificate** is sent to the device. To talk to the Intune service, you need this certificate.

Can we manage a Server Operating System with Intune?

No, Intune is not meant to handle servers. It is an **endpoint device management** solution. Support for servers is not likely to be added to Intune any time soon. But Intune can handle VDI tasks that are run on Windows 10 or 11 multi-session operating systems, which is a lot like server OS.

What are the options to onboard users and devices to Intune?

It's hard to answer this question again because it's not clear what it wants. If you need to, don't be afraid to ask for more information.

You can talk about requirements for training users like:

- The user must have an **Azure AD identity**.
- The user needs to have **Intune Licenses (Azure AD P1 for Conditional Access)**.

Also, give these answers to the question about adding devices to Intune:

- One of the device options for devices already connected to Intune is **Co-Management of Windows Devices.**
- Another option for adding devices to Intune is **Windows Autopilot**.
- Another way to set up Windows Azure AD Joined Devices is through **automatic enrollment**.
- Hybrid AD joined devices can also be added to Intune through **Intune Group Policy Enrollment**.
- Different ways are allowed by both Apple and Android that can be used to join **Apple and Android devices**. Signing up for personal devices is different from signing up for company-owned devices.

Does Intune admin have an option to go back to the previous version?

I don't think this is how SaaS works. You need to use the most recent working version of the portal. There is **NO option** to return to the Microsoft Intune service version that was used in the past. So, the answer is no, you can go back once you get the newest version of Azure. This also works for the Intune portal.

How do the User, Device, and Group Discoveries work in Intune?

Again, it doesn't matter how Users, Devices, and Groups are found for SaaS options like Intune. The reason for this is that the solution works very well with Azure AD devices, user accounts, and groups.

- Intune does not have its own user and group objects. Instead, it uses Azure AD users and groups directly.
- Intune also gets its device identities from Azure AD. However, the Intune service has its device objects that are closely linked to Azure AD device objects.

What are the concepts of collections and groups in Intune?

In contrast to SCCM groups, there is no such thing as an Intune collection. For Intune, there are no separate group items that can be used. Azure AD Groups (User and Device) are used by Intune. When the Intune Silverlight portal was in use, some groups were just for it. But there is something called "Intune Filtering Rules' ' that has to do with collections in Intune. This is like the idea of a group in SCCM. Intune's screening rules can keep devices from being assigned to a program or policy.

You can also use Azure AD Groups for the following rollout options:

a)   **Assigned/Static User AAD Groups**
b)   **Assigned/Static Device AAD Groups**
c)   **Dynamic User AAD Groups**
d)   **Dynamic Device AAD Groups**

What is Windows Auto Enrollment?

When Windows devices join or register with Azure Active Directory, you can set up a policy in Intune to automatically add them to Intune control. All MDM companies, like Intune, AirWatch, and others, can use this service or solution from Azure AD. The auto-enrollment makes it easier to handle company data on the Windows devices that your workers use.

What is Windows Autopilot? Is it a Replacement for SCCM OSD?

Microsoft gives you Windows Autopilot as a server as part of Endpoint Manager to make the **Windows out of Box Experience (OOBE) easier.** The service that helps with OS rollout is not Windows Autopilot. Any operating system can't be put on Windows devices by this service. Autopilot works on top of a device's new operating system to make the first login process easier (OOBE). That being said, you need a new way to rebuild the operating systems of devices, etc.

How to Onboard Devices into Windows Autopilot?

Adding devices to Windows Autopilot can be done in three different ways, which are:

- Add the Deployment Profile and upload the Device Hash.
- As part of the buying process, ask the sellers to add the new devices to Autopilot services.
- If the devices are already in tune, use the "**Convert all targeted devices to Autopilot**" option.

When the listed devices run the Windows out of Box Experience (OOBE) again, they will run the given Autopilot scenario with the experience.

Where can you check the Windows Autopilot Sync status with Intune Service?

You need to go to the Intune Admin (Intune) portal and log in. Then, go to:

- Go to **Devices > Enroll Devices > Windows Enrollment**
- Go to "**Windows Autopilot Deployment Program**" and click on "**Devices**" to see if Windows Autopilot and MS Intune are in sync!

You can find out more about the sync by looking at the **last sync** request and the **last successful sync.** Between Intune and Autopilot Service, you can also sync them by hand.

Where can you check the SCCM and Intune Sync? Cloud Attach Status?

Helpdesk and other teams can handle devices from the Intune portal with the help of SCCM Cloud Attach, which helps to sync SCCM devices with Intune. From the Intune portal, you can also do things remotely for SCCM clients.

Here are the steps you can take to see how SCCM Cloud Attach Sync is working with Intune:

- Log in to the **Intune Admin Center**. Find **Tenant Administration** and click on it.
- Click on **Connectors and Tokens**. Then, click on **Microsoft Endpoint Configuration Manager**.

Here you can see if the link between SCCM and Intune is healthy and the last time it successfully synced. You can also see information like the Name of the SCCM Server, the Site code, the Site full version, the Site mode, and the Support ID.

SCCM Cloud Attach sync SCCM DB with Intune?

The "**SCCM Cloud attach**" is a design that lets you connect whenever you need to. It's not true that Microsoft is copying the whole SCCM database to the Intune service!!

What are the Remote Assistance options available for Intune Managed devices?

In the Intune Admin Center portal, you can find some options for Remote Assistance. Online Help is the name of Microsoft's answer to online help. This works very well with Intune, Azure AD, and other things. It's not included in the Intune service or license, but you do need to buy a separate license for the Remote Help option. TeamViewer is another online help tool that is built into the Intune portal. There is also an extra license needed for this online help service.

Which is the recommended method to create Intune Policies?

Again, this is a hard Intune Interview Question because the real answer is "It depends." There are various ways to make policies in Intune. The Endpoint Security page is where you need to make security policies that focus on protection. From this page, you can also make and handle other security policies, like Defender Antivirus, Encryption, Firewall, and more. For all the different types of devices, like Windows, iOS/iPadOS, and macOS, Intune policies must be made using the Settings Catalog process.

Explain the patching mechanism in Intune

The whole process of Intune updating is based on Windows Update for Business (WUfB). For Intune patching to work, you don't need a WSUS server. It's easy and not as complicated to patch with Intune as with SCCM. In Intune, you don't have to pick and make monthly patch packages. Policies for feature and quality changes are all that are necessary. If you choose the "Quality updates for Windows 10 and later" option, you can make policies for quickly deploying patches. The policies in this section make it easier for clients to get in touch with the WUfB service in the cloud and apply patches. The WUA server takes care of the update process on the client side.

What is a Windows Autopatch patching mechanism? How is it different from the normal WUfB patching method?

Microsoft added a new service called Windows Autopatch to make the jobs of IT administrators a lot easier. Microsoft Autopatch is a cloud service that changes Windows, Microsoft 365 Apps for business, Microsoft Edge, and Microsoft Teams automatically. The Intune license does not come with a Windows AutoPatch license. That means you need to buy more licenses if you don't already have the right ones. Windows Autopatch takes care of the following rings automatically:

1. **Modern Workplace Devices – Test**
2. **Modern Workplace Devices – First**
3. **Modern Workplace Devices – Fast**
4. **Modern Workplace Devices – Broad**

What is the third-party application patching solution for Intune?

Intune will soon be able to fix third-party apps. But you need an extra license for this. It's not part of the basic license for Intune. SCCM has a built-in third-party repair option, but it is very basic. However there are third-party app developers, like PatchMyPC and ManageEngine, that can help get all the third-party fixes to the Intune portal automatically.

What are Intune App Protection or DLP Policies?

Mobile Application Management (MAM) solutions work hand-in-hand with DLP or App security policies. To control only the business apps instead of the whole device, this is the way to go. App security policies are rules that make sure an organization's data stays safe and under control in a managed app, even if Intune isn't used to monitor the device. Most of the time, the Intune App security policies are used with iOS and Android devices. The Intune App Protection Policy can be a list of things that you can't do or that are being watched. This policy can also help keep data from moving from work apps to personal ones.

Can Intune protect Enterprise App Data without managing the device itself?

Yes, you can use Intune App security, DLP, or MAM policies to keep business app data safe. You need to wrap an app with the Intune App SDK to use the Intune App security policy for those app. Around 100 sellers have already added Intune App Protection policies to their apps in the Google Play and Apple Play shops. Things like MS Office Apps, Adobe Acrobat, and more are examples. You can control and protect apps and data with Intune App Protection Policies without registering iOS, Android, or Windows devices in MDM.

Can you assign Intune App Protection Policies to Azure AD Device Groups?

Azure AD Device Groups can have Intune App Protection policies added to them. But it's not a good idea to give the device group an app security policy. The Azure AD User groups should be given the Intune App security policies. The goal of the Intune App security policies is to "just" handle business apps and data, not the devices that users use. Putting these policies on Azure AD Device groups doesn't make sense in that case.

Is it Mandatory to enroll devices to use MAM or Intune App Protection Policies?

No, you don't have to sign up the device for Intune to use MAM or Intune app security policies. You can give these kinds of policies to people, and they will still work without **device enrollment**.

Can you automatically migrate AD Group Policies to Intune Cloud Policies, and how do you?

You can move supported AD Group Policies to Intune Cloud Policies, yes. Group Policy Analytics is a new tool from Microsoft that lets you move on-premise group policies to policies in the Intune Settings Catalog. You can look at your on-premises GPOs with Group Policy Analytics to see how much current management help you have. Click "**Import**" to start the analysis, and click "Migrate" when you're ready to replace your old choices with new ones.

- Export GPOs into XML
- Import Group Policy XML to Intune
- Analyze the policies to determine whether these GPOs are MDM-compatible or not
- Migrate **GPOs** to **Intune Settings Catalog policies**

Conclusion

Microsoft Intune is like a superhero for businesses trying to keep their computers, phones, and tablets safe and organized. It helps bosses and IT folks make sure that all the devices people use for work are protected and follow the rules. With Intune, companies can set up rules to make sure only the right people can access important stuff, like company files and emails. It also helps them manage which apps are allowed on work devices and keeps everything updated and running smoothly. Think of Intune as the friendly neighborhood watch for your company's tech stuff. It's there to keep an eye out for trouble and make sure everything stays safe and in order. So, if you're in charge of tech at your company, Intune could be your new best friend!

INDEX

I

J

K

L

M

U

V

W

Z

Made in the USA
Las Vegas, NV
12 October 2024